DOGLEG MADNESS

⊙ ⊙ ⊙

MIKE BRYAN

⊙ ⊙ ⊙

DOGLEG MADNESS

THE ATLANTIC MONTHLY PRESS
NEW YORK

•

Copyright © 1988 by Mike Bryan

Portions of this book have appeared in different form in *Golf Magazine*, *Connoisseur*, *The Boston Globe Magazine*, and *Diversion*.

Published simultaneously in Canada
Printed in the United States of America
FIRST PAPERBACK EDITION

LIBRARY OF CONGRESS CATALOGING-IN-PUBLICATION DATA

BRYAN, MIKE.
    DOGLEG MADNESS / MIKE BRYAN.
    1. GOLF—UNITED STATES.   I. TITLE.
GV981.B79   1987
796.352′0973—DC19   87-28947

ISBN 0-87113-330-X

Design by Laura Hough

The Atlantic Monthly Press
19 Union Square West
New York, NY 10003

FIRST PRINTING

For Myrtle,
and in memory of
Bailey, Corene, and Henry

ACKNOWLEDGMENTS

Out of the dozens of golfers who have helped form my understanding of the game, such as it is, over the past twenty years, I especially thank George Peper, Robin McMillan, John Andrisani, and everyone else on the staff at *Golf Magazine*, and Lew Fishman, who has moved to *Golf Digest*.

On the PGA Tour, Ben Crenshaw, Peter Jacobsen, Johnny Miller, Jack Nicklaus, Andy North, Mac O'Grady, and caddie Russell Steib have been more than helpful. Likewise, Executive Director Frank Hannigan and Dean Knuth at the United States Golf Association. At ABC Sports, Cathy Rehl and Jim Jennett went out of their way to help me at Shinnecock Hills.

In Ozona, Texas, everyone was kind and generous to a fault, especially Dick Webster and Horses Williams, my hosts for the weekend in West Texas. Bill and Glenys McMillan, my hosts in Prestwick, Scotland, and John Bochel in Nairn made up for the lack of sunshine over there.

Another special thanks is due my family, with all of whom I've played golf: my father, mother, brother, uncle, father-in-law, mother-in-law, brother-in-law, sister-in-law, and nephew.

Most important of all for this book may be the famous foursome from Brooklyn: Peter Chester, Steve Gaskins, Gene Keogh, and Ted Wheeler. Without the fun of our outings to revive my interest in golf, this book would not have been written.

Finally, I thank Tom Quinn, who helped focus the idea, and my editor Gary Fisketjon, my agent Joe Spieler, and my wife Patty for their help with the various drafts of the book.

1

About ten years ago when my golf game was in one of its periodic wrecked states, I finally took a lesson, the first of my life, from a teaching pro with a good reputation in Austin, Texas. He watched me hit balls for a while and then offered one suggestion. "You might close up your hands a little," he said.

What he meant was, "I don't know, son. I don't know why you hit so many bad shots."

With most golfers, you know. They look terrible. Good golf requires a fulcrum, a center. Most players have no idea where theirs is, or might be. My problem was different. For all those years I'd had a fine-looking golf swing, sweet, pure, and untutored: swing it back, swing it through. One reason I lost interest and quit the game several times was the discrepancy between that pretty swing and my awful scores.

I've stood on the tee in the middle of a round shooting bogey or worse and been told by my partner, a golfer I didn't know until that day, "You sure have a beautiful swing."

I've been knee-deep in weeds trying to hack my ball back to landscaping and heard a player murmur, "He sure has a beautiful swing."

I've played with my brother who doesn't play at all and lost to his funky style.

I've played beautifully for six holes, hitting fairways and

1

greens, only to pull-hook my next drive, scuff my approach, lose my head and fail to execute another shot all day, and finish with a score, I believe, of 105. Par is 72. With his swing, a desecration of the game: that's what I imagined my partner muttering as we walked off the eighteenth green.

I think of Benjy, the simpleton, who, in the first paragraph of *The Sound and the Fury*, is enjoying the game of golf: "Through the fence, between the curling flower spaces, I could see them hitting. They were coming toward where the flag was and I went along the fence. Luster was hunting in the grass by the flower tree. They took the flag out, and they were hitting. Then they put the flag back and they went to the table, and he hit and the other hit. Then they went on, and I went along the fence."

Luster is the black boy who takes care of Benjy and finds golf balls for him. Benjy enjoys golf—the swing of the club and the flight of the ball, the wind blowing the clouds, and the ball itself, white on the green or heavy in his hand. (The golf ball is the purest of them all: the smallest, hardest, whitest, heaviest in feel, and it goes the farthest.)

I, too, was attracted to golf by the cool feel of it, even on the hottest Texas days when sweat threatened at six A.M. I loved the beauty of the courses, the easy pace of play, the long solitudes between shots, and, of course, my perfectly natural golf swing.

For all those years, my golf game thrived on the esteem garnered by that swing. I parred every hole on the scorecard of aesthetics, and bogeyed most of them on the real one. I never moved much beyond Benjy's simple grasp of the game.

After a sip of water from a paper cup and a few quiet words with his somber caddie, pro golfer Bob Eaks rotated on the golf ball with his long, smooth swing and hit a big drive. The time was precisely seven A.M. on Thursday morning, June 12, 1986, and that was the first shot of the national championship at the Shinnecock Hills Golf Club in Southampton, New York.

Eaks's tee ball was a draw—the controlled right-to-left shot that is, for many good players, the natural result of proper swing mechanics executed by strong arms and hands. But too much hand action will produce a hook—a wild shot screaming off to the left—and golfers who draw the ball are forever susceptible to streaks of hooking. Ben Hogan battled a hook for years, calling it the rattlesnake in his left pocket. The average hacker, however, has all the opposite problems. He possesses neither the proper swing mechanics nor strong hand action, so his effort merely slides the clubhead across the ball and the result is the weak, left-to-right slice. Hook, slice, draw, fade, pull, push, chili dip, top, shank, and so on: rare is the long, straight shot in golf.

The first fairway at Shinnecock Hills is a dogleg right, so the fairway bending to the right and Bob Eaks's shot bending to the left followed two different vectors from the elevated tee. To compensate, he had to aim his drive far out over the right rough—a raw field of fescue grasses, berry bushes, splashes of sand, and disturbed birds—and draw the ball back across the angle of the dogleg. Compounding his problem on this gray and blustery day on eastern Long Island was the strong breeze sweeping across the golf course from the east, from behind the golfer, on the first hole, adding distance to the drive but thereby increasing the chances of hitting the ball too far, through the fairway and into the rough on the left side. On Thursday, Eaks had to start the ball even farther to the right— farther over the trouble.

A more prudent drive on this hole would have been a left-to-right fade that followed the dogleg of the fairway, vectors in

3

sync. The first fairway sets up perfectly for most of the pros on the tour today, who fade the ball because it's easier to control than the draw. Maybe Eaks can hit a fade, maybe he can't. On Thursday morning he chose the theoretically riskier but apparently more reliable draw for his first shot in his first appearance in the national championship.

Thwack! The ball soared far out over the right rough with a rapid counterclockwise spin, turned slowly to the left, waved good-bye to all the trouble below, and dropped onto the fairway left of center. Only six seconds had elapsed, but they created some mild drama as the couple of hundred golf fans already on the course joined Eaks in following the flight of the ball through the windy air. Now the ball shined whitely on the green grass and the fans applauded briefly. Most of them had known nothing about this young professional. Now they knew that he hit a long ball—and a draw. Eaks handed the driver to his caddie and received a brief compliment, looked once more with satisfaction at his trophy far down the fairway, then stood impassively beside his black-and-white Titleist golf bag wearing his black-and-white cool-weather ensemble and watched while his two playing partners hit their drives. For the moment, Bob Eaks was a happy man.

Playing with him was a Canadian, Thomas Cleaver, who also played a draw on the hole, but weakly, and his ball fizzled into the left rough. The third member of the group, Wayne Smith, an Australian wearing khaki pants and scuffed brown golf shoes—bush dress—either mishit his shot, also a draw, or misjudged the distances and angles, or both. In all probability it was a mishit, but the strong wind from the east might have fooled him. The pros don't like to play a golf course in one wind in the practice rounds, only to have it switch around on them during the tournament. At their level of skill, different winds create different golf courses, and that's what happened on Thursday at Shinnecock Hills.

Whatever the case, Smith's ball sailed way right and never made it back to the fairway; didn't even come close. Silence greeted that shot, and the large gallery moved out— large only because most of those fans were heading onto the golf course, where they would promptly abandon this obscure trio in order to watch the famous players who would come along later. The pairings in the Open for the first two rounds on Thursday and Friday are based on caliber: the big names on the tour play together, likewise the lesser lights, likewise the pros who haven't even made it to the tour but have qualified for this tournament. Thus ninety percent of the crowd would follow the celebrated ten percent of the three-somes, and as many fans as could jam in would follow just one group: Jack Nicklaus's. He would have the biggest galleries of the tournament, thousands of fans, no matter how well he played. Eaks, Cleaver, Smith, and their unknown confreres would have the smallest: no one at all, in fact, except for a wife, a friend, a straggler.

This is nothing new. Celebrity has a life of its own for golf fans, too. They go out to see golfers, not golf. If this phenomenon of the times needs an excuse, the game gives it a good one. After all, you don't see much golf at a tournament anyway, not as a percentage of the whole play for the day. A fan who parks himself at a good location beside a green early in the morning and stays until sunset will see exactly one-eighteenth of that day's golf, about as good as he could do. So why not watch somebody famous instead?

Nor is a round of golf all that exciting, per se. In tennis, one player pounds the ball past the other guy and leaves him sprawling at the net. In golf, there is no other guy. The competition is quiet. The shots are quiet. The game lacks the kinetic excitement of tennis or the team sports, with their conflict *mano a mano*.

Things don't get noisy—or deathly quiet—at a golf tournament until the final holes on Sunday, when victory is close and the importance of every shot is patently clear. And in one other instance: when we care deeply about the golfer. Then the player is in competition with himself—past exploits, inevitable approaching decline—and therefore with the hopes and fears of his fans. Isn't this conflict *mano a mano,* too? Watching the revered Jack Nicklaus shoot a 75 means more to most fans than watching Bob Eaks or Thomas Cleaver shoot a 65. Watching Nicklaus shoot a 65—well, just note the universal joy that greeted the Golden Bear's victory at The Masters two months before the Open. My wife and I were watching that tournament on television, and at one point early in the broadcast the action was focused on other golfers playing the ninth hole. As the commentators were describing those events, a deep and heartfelt roar issued from fans massed elsewhere on Augusta National, and even on TV it seemed thunderous. My wife said, "That's Jack," and she was right. A birdie for Nicklaus, and he went on to shoot a 65 that Sunday to win.

In any event, neither Eaks nor Cleaver nor Smith was likely to shoot a 65 on Thursday at Shinnecock Hills. After their drives on the first hole, Eaks had the best chance—his big blow left him a simple half-wedge to the green—but he was too careful with the shot and left the ball twelve feet short of the flag. He scowled as he walked up to the green: The half-wedge should be boilerplate for the pros, right on the money.

Cleaver located his ball in the heavy grass. Not surprisingly, his approach iron from that lie ended up in a bunker short of the green. Wayne Smith caught a workable lie in a sandy patch in the right rough—the ball could just as easily have been unplayable—and hit a beautiful iron to the green, six or seven feet from the hole. The net result of the approach shots was that Smith, the player in potentially the worst position off the tee, had the best chance for a birdie. He missed the putt. Eaks missed his putt. Cleaver blasted from the sand to within a yard of the cup and made the short one. Three pars. The volunteer accompanying the players and holding aloft a small scoreboard posted an *E* for "even par" by each of the names. The first threesome of the championship had proved once again that with golf and every other good game, it's not how, but how many. Eaks's long, accurate drive wasn't rewarded because of the nervous wedge shot. Cleaver's bad drive and difficult iron were saved by an excellent explosion from the bunker. Smith's bad drive caught a lucky lie, but he couldn't make the short putt to capitalize on the break.

Good shots unrewarded, bad shots unpunished: Whole careers have been marked by these inequities. A journeyman named Orville Moody couldn't win on the pro tour despite accurate, often uncanny shotmaking because he just couldn't putt (with the exception of one weekend in 1969, when he putted well enough to win the U.S. Open). Tom Watson hit plenty of crooked drives and irons but thrived as the best player in the game in the late seventies and early eighties, all on the strength of great chipping and putting. He wouldn't have won without that wonderful touch around the greens—and he isn't winning much without it now.

Ben Hogan hated this state of affairs; he wanted great shots rewarded and bad ones penalized. Hogan and a few other like-minded players have even recommended alternative scoring systems that award points for shotmaking—fairways and greens hit "in regulation." Putts would count for less, or for nothing at all. Keeping score on the first hole at Shinnecock Hills under a Hogan system, Eaks would have been leading with two points (fairway and green in regulation), Smith following with one point (green in regulation), and Cleaver scoreless.

Hogan's game never would have made it. Golf would have died aborning, right there on the dunes of Scotland. It's an old truth: The great games (golf and baseball, mainly) mirror the unfairness and haphazardness of our lives, then top off the punishment with the incongruous objectivity of a final score. Though it's a joke, we must like it—perhaps even need it. We play, don't we, and nobody is forcing us to. Without this inherent craziness, a game is merely a demonstration, an exercise like marksmanship or bowling. Golf could be played like that, but not many people would enjoy it. We want the opportunity to recover from the sliced drive with a skillful second shot or a long and lucky putt. We tolerate the bad break (in our rational moments) because we might be in line for a good one.

From this point of view, a footrace isn't fair at all: One of the runners is always faster than the others.

But I could beat Jack Nicklaus on the golf course—for a hole or two—with luck. *That* is what I call fairness.

Fair or not, Eaks, Cleaver, and Smith walked to the second tee all even at par. As they played that long, tough par-three hole, a full-blown Nor'easter was gearing up across Long Island, and it would ruin the golf scores of most of the best players in the world.

Bob Eaks's tee shot on two was a solid stroke, but the crosswind pushed the ball into a terrible lie on the edge of a bunker left of the green; *in* the bunker would have been better. Wayne Smith didn't reach the putting surface. Thomas Cleaver hit the only accurate shot to the green, where he lit his first cigarette of the day in celebration and then sank the birdie putt. A fan sitting in the bleachers behind the green whistled the birdie call. *Tweet tweet tweet tweet*. A red 1 was immediately posted by Cleaver's name. One under par, he was leading the national championship.

Smith bogeyed the hole. Eaks hacked his ball onto the

putting surface, took two putts for a bogey, tossed his putter at his golf bag, and stalked up the small hill to the third tee, where he turned his back on his partners down on the second green (poor form), lit *his* first cigarette of the round, and stared downwind into the woods, no longer a happy man.

Then he pulled his drive into the light rough on the third hole. The ball was sitting up—a decent lie—but he pulled that shot, too, and watched as the ball hopped underneath a bush to the left of the green. Now Eaks had a long walk in which to consider the missed birdie opportunity on the first green, the bad break with his lie on the second hole, and the flustered swing that had just pulled the ball twice on the third hole. Or maybe he tried to think about something else; the storm over the course was growing more entertaining by the moment. A lot has been written about the loneliness of the golfer as he trudges to his next shot or waits to putt, and much of this speculation is too reverential; half the time the pros are scoping out the women in the gallery or following the advice of the venerable pro Walter Hagen, given decades ago: "Never hurry, never worry, and be sure to smell the flowers along the way."

But Bob Eaks did look lonely as he walked down the left side of the fairway toward his ball. Only three holes into this windblown round and he was already in danger of losing his bearings. It can happen fast on a golf course.

Greenside, he crawled under the bush to identify his ball. Every pro makes some little identifying mark on his golf balls before a round. This mark and the manufacturer's label assure that he doesn't incur a two-stroke penalty for hitting the wrong one. The ball under the bush was his, all right, but he couldn't hit it with any kind of plausible swing, and another rule prevented him from breaking away branches in order to facilitate his swing. Eaks stared down at the bush and the ball, tried one stance, stared down again, set up with another stance, then backed away again, probably considering whether to declare the ball unplayable and thereby present himself with another set of options, none of them good. (To all appearances a straightforward affair, tournament golf is nevertheless regulated by 110 pages of rules, many of them devoted to penalties.)

Any of the unplayable lie options would probably cost him a double bogey; if he could somehow advance the ball from under the bush with a legitimate stroke, he'd have a decent chance of salvaging a bogey. Pros can tolerate a bogey now and then, and certainly on a difficult course in bad conditions, when some are inevitable. Double bogeys are terrible at all times.

Forty yards from the scene (as close as the gallery ropes allowed on this particular hole), a man standing next to me observed Eaks's deliberations through binoculars and called the play-by-play. Finally, Eaks took a stance and chopped at the ball, which hopped out of the bush and into the light rough. He then chipped well and sank the short bogey putt. A golfer can go one of two ways after such a hole: Be thankful for escaping with the bogey, or remain angry over his bad shots and bad luck, forgetting that there isn't much bad luck in the middle of the green. After his second bogey in a row, Eaks appeared to choose the second option. He was steaming, and the man with the binoculars was gratified. Golf fans want to see excellence from their heroes, but they also enjoy seeing the other pros screw up and get mad. Those misfortunes bring closer together the two levels of skill that are otherwise so dissimilar. A double bogey, a *triple* bogey: The average golfer can really relate to that futility.

Wayne Smith was inexplicably short of the green with his second shot—but maybe not so inexplicably: Short was better than long, with those bushes so close behind. Although Smith is one of those golfers who simply look like they have a good

touch around the green—soft hands on the grip is part of it—
he proceeded to skull the chip over the green, hit another bad
one back, then not come close with his putt. Double bogey.

Thomas Cleaver missed a short putt for par and his red
number disappeared from the board, and there would be no
more under-par red for these players this day. I was ready to
bet on it when the squall that had been spitting rain for two
holes finally opened up on the fourth. Players, caddies, and
the well-prepared fans hustled into their rain gear, and some
of the gallery wore silly grins. Conditions were so bad they
were fun for the few.

At last, Bob Eaks got a good break on the fourth hole. His
drive was in the rough, but he had a shot at the green and
pulled it off. Wayne Smith drove right, too, but he didn't find
any luck over there, and by the time he made it to the green
I'd lost count of the strokes. He ended up with a six, another
double bogey. Now *his* was the round that appeared to be in
jeopardy: five over par after four holes. Cleaver sank a 5 footer,
and I knew it wasn't for a birdie. Par or bogey? He smiled:
par.

Eaks's hopes lifted noticeably after his good approach
shot from the rough. His stride had a little spring in it. Maybe
he could turn things around with a few pars. After all, he was
only two over par, and if he could stabilize and shoot in the
mid 70s, even the upper 70s, he'd be okay. All the scores in
the first round would be high. But then he three putted. On
the second hole Eaks had tossed his putter in anger after the
frustrating bogey; now he just slumped off the fourth green,
dispirited.

After four holes, the first threesome in the tournament
stood like this: Cleaver even par, Eaks three over, and Smith
five over.

A triumph for Thomas Cleaver, and he looked positively
happy even though the wind was blowing harder, the rain was

colder, and the clouds were thick in all directions. The storm seemed to be settling in, and it was time for the players to do the same, preparing themselves for the inevitable windblown shots and subsequent bogeys. They couldn't look for help from the officials: If the rain didn't blind them and if there was no lightning, they would play all day. Wayne Smith looked okay despite his high numbers. Bob Eaks appeared stricken.

But all that could change on the fifth hole, much less the thirteen others to follow. A grinning man who hunkered beneath a bright red umbrella exclaimed to one and all, "This isn't TV. This is real life!" I had to agree. Even after shooting 105, even after quitting, I've always felt that way about it.

2

I grew up with the game of golf, caddieing for, then occasionally playing with my father on a layout sunk down with the bayous and mosquitoes on the industrial east side of Houston. The geography is important only because there aren't many golf courses on the wrong side of any town. Or many golfers. We lived on the higher and drier west side, and drove for an hour every Saturday at sunrise in order to be first off, or close to it, with our regular foursome. Home by one to mow the lawn.

The Texaco Country Club was a company-owned facility, built on cheap land with cheap labor—including the employees' own, organized into work parties on weekends back around the Depression. By the time my father was transferred to Houston in 1957, the amenities at the club included a swimming pool and a white cinder-block clubhouse, and our stable postwar family of four sometimes returned to the club on Saturday evenings for dinner, dancing, and standing around.

Texaco was, and still is, a short, eighteen-hole track featuring a bayou, some ponds, wide fairways lined with pine trees, and small, humpbacked greens, a few of them protected by a flat bunker or two. The course looked easy, but you had to stay in the fairways, and the little greens were hard to hold with an approach shot. Most players tried to roll the ball on.

Texaco wasn't a great golf course and there wasn't much great golf played there. My father speaks for most of the regulars at Texaco when he says, "I've been an eighteen handicapper as long as I can remember."

That's bogey golf, just about the national average. Bogey golf; I either inherited or learned that trait.

The golfers I grew up with were weekend enthusiasts without great pretensions or ambitions on the course that I could see. Those fathers grew up during the Depression, worked their way through a state-supported college, married, went off to the world war and then the Korean War, sired their children as the opportunities arose, came home from the wars, and went to work for a safe company in order to support that family. Texaco was such a company. On the west side of Houston in the fifties and sixties, getting rich wasn't necessarily part of the plan. There was money around, but not too much. For one thing, there was too much oil. Those were the days of the price wars. At the corner Texaco station where I worked, gas got as low as fifteen cents. We gave away or sold at deep discount a wide variety of enticements, including glasses, beer-holders, fire-chief hats, toy tankers, and Texaco trucks.

I played less and less golf as my gas-pumping teenage years went by, and then quit altogether when I went off to college in New York City. It was five years before I swung a club again, when I returned to Texas to work. A friend suggested I accompany him to the practice range one evening, and I can still see the surprise register on his face as my first swings with his loaned clubs produced good shots. I can also see his chagrin after I caught the 3-wood on the heel and snapped off the clubhead. It flew out into the darkness and we had to call a cease fire on the range while we hunted for it. But I started playing again and played a lot for several years, then less and less for the next few, and finally I left my clubs behind, with no feeling of regret, when I moved back to New York. I knew what golf was like on the public courses in the five boroughs of the city, and although I had enjoyed the sunrise services with my father, fifteen years later I wasn't up for it: lining up at four A.M. to play a hacked-up layout in a six-hour round with guys I didn't know.

But then I made some friends who played golf, and my clubs arrived from Texas two weeks later. Almost every Saturday that summer the four of us drove an hour and a half from our apartments in Brooklyn to play a good semiprivate course in northern New Jersey. Now the course was on the right side of town, and I wasn't.

Really hooked again, I wrote a Sunday magazine piece all about the game for a Boston newspaper. The editor of *Golf Magazine,* one of the two major golf magazines, read it and liked it. I was looking for some free-lance work, but George Peper invited me to his Madison Avenue office for a job interview instead. We talked for about an hour and his last question was, "How good are you?" I knew he had been afraid to ask. I looked him straight in the eye and said, "Not very. Sometimes I don't break 100." He gulped and hired me anyway.

I played more than I ever had—on an expense account, no less. My business card was a ticket to all but the most finicky clubs. I played at Winged Foot and Quaker Ridge, two jewels north of Manhattan in Westchester County. I played Wild Dunes in South Carolina against a squad of British and Irish golf writers in an annual promotion called the World Writers' Cup, and I still have the engraved putter and embossed travel bag to prove it. I went to pro tournaments all over: The Masters, the Open, the PGA, and many more. I chatted with all the top players, Nicklaus and Palmer and

Watson and Trevino; with Gene Sarazen, Tommy Bolt, and other characters from the past; with Robert Trent Jones and Pete Dye and other famous golf-course architects.

Most of them returned my phone calls.

After two years, I quit the job and the game. That was in 1984. I'd been as committed to golf as to anything, and the record speaks for itself: umpteen jobs and thirty or so years of quitting and playing. In my case golf is more than a game: It's another tune on the fiddle, a tune I admired—even loved—but refused to learn well. I played as I lived, haphazardly.

"The best lack all conviction, while the worst / Are full of passionate intensity." Yeats's gloomy (and by now trite) assessment suited me just fine when I first read the poet twenty years ago. Lacking all conviction myself, at least I was in good company. But then Robert Kennedy cried out (quoting Edmund Burke, I believe), "The only thing necessary for the triumph of evil is for good men to do nothing," and I looked at myself again, a good man (college kid, actually) doing nothing, fiddling as my country burned, in the ghettos, on the campuses, across the Pacific. I had tried to do something my first year at Columbia College, signing up for a hospital program in Harlem. I forget what the work was but clearly remember the bottle hurled against my back late one fall afternoon. I chickened out.

My next stab at commitment was a black armband of mourning worn after the cops rioted on campus in 1968, galloping horses down Broadway at three A.M., pinning students against the wall. I hadn't been inside the occupied buildings, of course. The famous radical leader Mark Rudd—by the luck of the draw my freshman roommate two years earlier—told me one day during the takeover, as I loitered by the sundial and he rushed off to some negotiation, that he had no idea what was happening, or why.

Passionate intensity? I couldn't believe it of any of them.

The events were more than a panty raid, but a good deal less than a revolution. Calling it a year, I accepted my "pass" grades and flew home early to Texas, where I was greeted as some kind of hero. My expensive Ivy League college had been torn apart by demonstrations, live on network television. I was in the crowds. My former roommate, my friend, was a radical leader of international renown. The sixties had happened to me.

But they had left me high and dry. I had seen what happened when the best and the brightest did act with all conviction: Vietnam. That was a narrow view, perhaps, but the best available to me at the time. Then General Patton looked down on the carnage of some battlefield and said in his movie, "Compared with war, all other human endeavor shrinks to insignificance." A few scenes later, at another killing ground, he added, "God help me, but I love it so."

Conviction good to the last drop, and I wanted none of it.

I couldn't keep the Socratics and the Sophists straight. My life was examined, all right, but so what? After graduation and a year of reading scripts for the movie business, I returned to Texas and joined VISTA (a universally understood acronym at the time, but less so now: Volunteers in Service to America). I worked with the chaplain in the Houston jail and "organized communities" on the east side of town, near the Texaco Country Club, in fact—a good, modest diet of conviction for a small planet.

Still pondering Yeats's dictum, I found it lacking. Some of my friends had passionate intensities, and they were hardly among "the worst." I was messing around with golf and books at an ever-advancing age while they healed the sick, defended the innocent, and fueled the national economy with their enterprise.

In the movie *Caddyshack*, a comedy about golf (and the only movie about the game in many years), the off-the-wall par shooter played by Chevy Chase delivers advice to his young caddie and pupil, who's trying to win a golf scholarship at the annual caddie's tournament. "Danny," Chase says solemnly, "see your future . . . be your future . . . make your future."

Or, as André Malraux wrote, "It does not matter what has been made of us. What matters is what we ourselves make of what has been made of us."

In my case, the answer to Malraux's challenge was inescapable and simple enough: I had made almost nothing of my talents. I hadn't even identified them.

I realize now that it had been all over between me and the magazine job six months before I quit. I was playing worse and worse; my swing didn't even look good anymore. The streaks of merely acceptable shots got so short I couldn't pretend I was on to something. They were flukes, a product of the odds, not talent. Then I hit rock bottom at a staff outing at the Westchester Country Club early in the summer.

I had hit a few good shots to start the round, then two really good ones on a par five. That left me with a half-wedge to the green, and there was a time in my life, maybe fifteen years earlier, when I was a good wedge player. I could hit the ball as close to the flag as I could throw it. Suddenly I felt that way again at Westchester, thanks mainly to the second shot on that hole, a perfectly struck long iron that rocketed a hundred yards before my eyes caught up with it. I was irrationally inspired. I would do it again with the wedge. My boss, George Peper, was playing in my foursome, and I hoped he was watching.

I stepped up and swung—and shanked it. I stared in amazement as the ball caromed off to the right at a thirty- or forty- or fifty-degree angle—too damned many to count—and came to rest up on the side of a hill. I shanked that next shot, too. Those two blows are vivid in my memory, but I don't remember a thing that happened the rest of the day.

A golfer can smile and keep going after the chili dip, the topped ball, even the whiff, because there's a clear explanation for those embarrassments: He simply didn't keep his eye on the ball. The shank is different, sui generis. It comes out of nowhere and for no certain reason. The standard consolation—that the shank is almost a perfect swing—only makes matters worse, because it points out the inexplicable nature of both the shank and the game.

In my defense: While the half-wedge shot is boilerplate for the pros, it's a very shankable shot for amateurs, so much so that a couple of shank-proof wedges are on the market. The shank is a shot off the hosel of the clubshaft; the ball never reaches the face of the club. The prophylactic wedges warp the hosel into a position way behind the clubface so that it's impossible to hit the hosel first.

I say they're worth it because the shank kills the spirit of the human being. It's a curse. Johnny Miller once told me about a ball he shanked many years ago, and admitted that he'd seldom played a round thereafter—a final round in a tournament he had a chance of winning—in which he didn't wonder at some point, "Now you're not going to shank this shot, are you?" If the shank bored thusly into Miller's mind, what chance did I have? He who shanks the ball becomes an untouchable. His playing partners avert their eyes. George Peper saw my second shank, I believe, and he didn't want to talk about it. For an editor of a golf magazine, a shank is a desecration of the game: That's what I imagined he was thinking as we walked off the green.

Mike Bryan

I protest too much. Most of the seventeen and a half million amateur golfers in the United States, and millions more in Europe and the Far East, have no idea what my problem is, and don't care. The huge percentage of these golfers are hackers having fun—getting mad, but having fun. They look terrible swinging at the ball, the ball shoots off line somewhere, and that's fine. Most golfers aren't overly concerned with either the aesthetic or the actual scorecard, despite all the time and money spent on lessons and equipment. They'll *act* concerned when they record the double bogey and lose a two-dollar Nassau bet, but how can they be, really? They finished the round with 90 or 100 or worse, and they didn't have a prayer of 72, or anything close to par, to begin with.

Par is a three-lettered code, the double helix that has eluded us all these years. For amateur golfers, par is a hopeless quest—and quest is the right word. Playing any game without hope of excellence has all the earmarks of tilting at windmills. Not only do we play without hope, we play without Don Quixote's delusions. We feel the joyful anticipation on the opening tee as we ponder our first shot down the fairway, but we aren't deceived. The little white ball mesmerizes us with its black magic, and we dream—but we don't lie. We know what's in store for us.

Nobody would fish in a verifiably empty lake. Golfers must play for reasons beyond par. The secret of golf was expressed best and with the least mysticism by Robert Tyre Jones, Jr.—Bobby Jones, the peerless gentleman and masterful golfer of the twenties who won the Grand Slam in 1930 and then, at the age of twenty-eight, retired from competition without turning pro.

"On the golf course," Jones wrote, "a man may be the dogged victim of inexorable fate, be struck down by an appalling stroke of tragedy, become the hero of a side-splitting

20

comedy—any of these within a few hours, and all without having to bury a corpse or repair a tangled personality."

No wonder we play golf! Detractors of the game laugh at par and dismiss golf as ridiculous—*cow-pasture pool*. They have a point; the game is silly. But so are all our games. We have a way of taking inherently meaningless activities and consecrating them, demanding even a lifetime's obeisance. Golf is such a ritual, and we're its adherents.

What is the game? A little ball with hundreds of dimples (and more every year, as manufacturers devise new, improved configurations) is struck with the best-suited of fourteen clubs carried in a bag. Each club is cunningly designed to propel the ball on a designated flight path if perfectly struck, or on a horribly wrong tangent if just slightly misstruck. The action takes place on a specially landscaped terrain with eighteen closely mowed swaths of grass (the fairways), water, sand, trees, and unmowed grass (the rough), culminating in more closely mowed medallions of grass (the greens), in each of which is hidden a little hole. A flagstick in the hole is an aid to navigation.

Hit the ball into the hole. Do it in a prescribed and pitilessly few number of shots—par. That's all there is to it.

But we cannot shoot par! Our passion for this failing is expensive, time-consuming, and enormously frustrating. We should quit, and we do, but then we come back. I've played tennis and jogged and swum and bowled, but they're not the same. They're cheaper, quicker, and less frustrating, but where's the inexorable fate? The tragedy? The unfairness and haphazard luck and ill luck? The greens fee for the most humble golf course in the world purchases all this keen drama, and more.

Golfers persevere, that's about the best that can be said, inspired in our hopeless quest by the high priests of the game, the professionals. This weekend, almost every weekend, some pro will bank about $100,000 for winning a golf tournament (on the women's tour, somewhat less). First prize at Shinnecock Hills was $115,000. Many amateurs, if they could play so well just one time, would *pay* that kind of money.

And for the most part, thank goodness, the godlike pros aren't worried about inexorable fate. They just play golf, following the sun and warm weather, not venturing north of the Mason-Dixon line until May, retreating again in September. Players, caddies, families, support personnel, concessionaires, television crews, and reporters shift ground every week, just like the circus. Several hundred people make the move and they're hooked on the game, the travel, the anything-but-nine-to-five life-style.

Most of the pros are working for a living. Golf is their job. In 1986, forty-one of the pros would earn over $200,000 in official money, a good living even with their high expenses, but hundreds of pros—Eaks, Cleaver, Smith, and the like—have to hustle hard to break even with outings and pro-ams and perhaps even regular jobs. Dogged victims abound in the pro ranks.

Theirs, however, is not the pro game we see. The one we see is the commercial wonder created by a golfer named Palmer and an invention called television, boosted by another golfer named Nicklaus, and invigorated by such stars as Lee Trevino, Tom Watson, Seve Ballesteros, and Calvin Peete. All this business of stars and celebrity and aggrandizement, million-dollar tournaments and Thanksgiving weekend "skins" in which one putt may be worth hundreds of thousands of dollars, warps crazily around a game that is the mere livelihood of the invisible journeyman and the weekend diversion of the average amateur golfer.

The dogged victim sometimes wins the national championship. Sometimes he also wins the high handicapper's flight in the club championship. I'm not certain which golfer feels the greater sense of accomplishment and sheer joy. For the club golfer, the weekend player, golf is the opposite of work. It is escape and fantasy. The letters that come in to golf magazines about holes-in-one are instructive, and the experience (I gather) is epiphanic. One magazine awards certificates for verified aces. I received a letter from a man who posted a double eagle (two on a par five hole, and much harder than a hole-in-one) and claimed, a year after the feat, that he was still on a "natural high." He was wondering whether we would award a plaque for the accomplishment. (No.)

Bill Murray, the greenskeeper in *Caddyshack*, lops off neatly planted crysanthemums with his scythe while imagining that every cleanly struck blossom at Bushwood Country Club is a great shot in a fourth-round charge at The Masters. Murray (who really is a golf nut) calls the play-by-play: "Incredible Cinderella story . . . former greenskeeper . . . he holes the shot! He holes the shot!" That's the mind of the zealous amateur golfer, to whom the game might mean more than it does to the professional. I know it means a hell of a lot. Ask any golfer for the highlight of his experience with the game. The answer will *never* be some shot he saw a pro make, or a favorite player's victory, not even Jack Nicklaus's at The Masters. It will always be a golfing triumph of his own.

In June 1986 I was at Shinnecock Hills watching the U.S. Open. Three months later I was in Ozona, Texas, at the Ozona Invitational, an annual event that draws amateur golfers from all over West Texas to that little town on Interstate 10, about halfway between San Antonio and El Paso. The term *invitational* is not a self-congratulatory pat on the back. Any golfer with a bone fide 2 handicap can try to qualify for the U. S. Open, but that same excellent application would be rejected out of hand by the organizers of the Ozona tournament. The nine-hole course can accommodate only thirty-six four-man teams, and most of these teams, in part or in whole, seek to return year after year. The tournament is booked solid.

When I was a kid, I spent part of my summers in Ozona, visiting my grandparents in their house up on the hill above the hospital. My grandfather was the administrator of that Crockett County facility. Twenty-five years of golf later, I thought it would be enjoyable and perhaps instructive to return to West Texas and find players of every stripe performing on the challenging little nine-holer, golfers and layout alike about as far as they could be from the glare of the mass media that would dominate the proceedings at Shinnecock Hills (although the same can't be said for Ozona itself, which was the subject of a profile in *The Saturday Evening Post* in 1950). Competitive amateur golf in its purest form, I hoped, as it's played by the rank and file.

In the beginning, Shinnecock Hills and the pro game all golfers aspire to. At summer's end, Ozona and the game we play in real life. Godlike proficiency, human fallibility, and everything in between. Put this together with side trips to Scotland and other venues and I'd have it all, the truth about the game that has dogged me all these years. I wanted to find out why I now believe and will still believe on my dying day that par golf or some facsimile thereof would have confirmed for me as well as anything might have, including money or best-sellers or a trip to the moon, my capacity for commitment, achievement, and fulfillment.

Is that a silly notion, or a great one?

3

"This is not stellar golf," grumbled the fan beside me as we stood in line at the concession stand hidden in a copse between the fourth fairway and the seventh green at Shinnecock Hills. He was correct. We had seen mostly struggling golfers on Thursday morning. The scoreboards showed green numbers in profusion, getting higher by the hole. The players were over par for the same reason my acquaintance and I were purchasing hot chocolate instead of cold beer as the Nor'easter built up speed. These weren't frostbite conditions, but it was cold and I had a hunch that the United States Golf Association (USGA) officials who brought the Open to Shinnecock Hills were secretly delighted. On the first day of the event they already had what they wanted—something different.

Hot and sultry days are more usual for the Open, which is always played in mid-June. In 1964, at the Congressional Country Club outside of Washington, D. C., the heat and humidity on the golf course were absolutely dangerous, with readings on the blistered greens above 110 degrees, and that was back when the final thirty-six holes were played on one day. Ken Venturi staggered home the winner that year on the verge of heat prostration, shooting rounds of 66 and 70. He was followed by medical personnel for the final eighteen.

The sites for the Open are picked years in advance, and

they are usually the grand, tree-lined, inland golf courses of the Northeast (Winged Foot north of Manhattan and Baltusrol across the Hudson River, Oakmont outside Pittsburgh, Merion in Philadelphia, Oak Hill in Rochester, and Brookline near Boston) and the Midwest (Bellerive in St. Louis, Medinah in suburban Chicago, Inverness in Toledo, Ohio, and Oakland Hills near Detroit). Besides having great golf courses, these clubs also have the large membership required to handle the volunteer staffing and the capacious facilities to handle the galleries of thirty thousand spectators and their cars.

For years, USGA officials had cast a covetous eye on Shinnecock Hills, but just as quickly turned away. A wonderful, windy golf course in the Scottish-English tradition, it was a different kind of layout for the Open, but it was all wrong in vital respects. Elusive Shinnecock Hills, tucked away in a remote, exclusive summer resort served by a single road? It just wouldn't do.

It's too small. Merely three hundred fifty members, with only about half of them living in the area. Who will staff the Open?

It's only a part-time club, closed from Election Day to April 15, and preparation for the Open is a year-round job. The clubhouse isn't even heated, and the telephone is re-routed in the winter to the home of the club accountant.

It's ultra low profile. The members don't want the publicity or the hassles. Thousands of fans, temporary buildings, tents, and Port-o-sans strewn everywhere? Thousands of cars and vans and trailers clogging every available country road for miles around? Peanuts! Popcorn! Hot dogs!

Good Lord, man, get serious. We're a golf club, not a national park!

Nothing about Shinnecock Hills was right—except the golf course itself, always considered among the elite of the great underplayed, underpublicized layouts in the world, and untested by the pros. The game at Shinnecock Hills dates back to 1891, one year after the Americans William K. Vanderbilt and Edward S. Mead and the immigrant Scotsman Duncan Cryder observed Willie Dunn, one of several famous Scottish golfers in that family, hitting balls in Biarritz, the French resort. Vanderbilt remarked to his cronies (or so the story goes), "Gentlemen, this beats rifle shooting for distance and accuracy. It's a game I think would go in our country."

The three wealthy men returned to the States and Long Island to proselytize their friends, and they quickly signed up seventeen charter members who anted up one hundred dollars apiece. Shinnecock Hills was thus the first incorporated golf club in the country (other establishments claim to be the first club, period). Willie Dunn was brought over to design twelve holes on land purchased from the Shinnecock Indians. Members of that tribe sculpted the fairways and greens with horse-drawn scrapers. This humble beginning was the time-honored way for golf clubs to form. Sixty years later some ranchers in Ozona, Texas, started their club in similar fashion, and they also contributed their own manual labor. Now, however, almost all new golf courses are either resorts or private clubs set up by developers who sell lots along the fairways and operate the club facilities for a profit. Play enough of these standardized tracks, and you begin to look out for tricycles.

A separate nine holes were built at Shinnecock Hills for the ladies, but they refused to go along with this segregation and wouldn't play their course, setting a precedent for equality that carries through to this day: Shinnecock Hills might be the only exclusive private club in this country that allows women to play on the golf course at any time. Beatrix Hoyt was a member. The greatest woman amateur of her day, she won the Women's Amateur in 1896, '97, and '98.

At any rate, the original twelve holes at Shinnecock Hills

were expanded, and the resulting eighteen holes were, in
1896, the site of the second U. S. Open, won by Jim Foulis, a
Scottish pro playing out of the Chicago Golf Club. In that era,
the Open was a secondary tournament because professionals
weren't held in particularly high regard by the gentry of the
private clubs. The Amateur was the real national championship, and the second national Amateur was also held at
Shinnecock Hills. (As late as the 1920s in Great Britain,
professional golfers were not allowed to use the front door of
clubhouses. In 1920, at the British Open at Royal Cinque
Ports in Deal, the flashy Walter Hagen hired a Daimler limo
and parked it in front of the clubhouse, complete with chauf-
feur and liveried footman, and used that facility as his locker.
Two years later, he was invited into the clubhouse at Royal St.
George's in Sandwich but declined, and dined instead with
his pals in a nearby pub. He won the tournament.)

The original eighteen at Shinnecock Hills no longer exist.
A new course, just north of the old one, was designed and
built by William Flynn, opening for play in 1931. This was the
course coveted by the USGA for a modern-day Open, when,
needless to say, the relative importance of the Open and the
Amateur has been reversed, decisively and permanently.

First, however, something on a smaller scale was planned
for Shinnecock Hills, and the club agreed to host the 1977
Walker Cup Match, the biennial contest between the best
amateur golfers of America and Britain. The Americans won
the matches, 16-8, and no player, including several college
stars on their way to the pros, matched par for any nine holes,
much less eighteen.

That impressive showing by the golf course settled the
matter. Some way simply had to be found to take the big one
to Shinnecock Hills, and negotiations commenced in 1980. If
the club members couldn't staff the committees, the USGA
would find the volunteers and run the tournament itself, just

as the Royal and Ancient Golf Club runs the British Open every year. If traffic and crowds were deemed a problem, the USGA would conduct a study and let the results dictate the number of cars allowed on the roads and fans on the course; if necessary, this would be a televised Open. (In the end, attendance was limited to eighteen thousand fans.) The members' pride in their golf course was massaged, and the USGA offered them $175,000 and a share of the receipts.

An agreement was concluded in 1981. Five years later, I was buying hot chocolate in the middle of June. Refreshment in hand, I doubled back on the front nine to pick up the first celebrity grouping of the day: Greg Norman, fresh from his loss to Jack Nicklaus on the final hole of The Masters; Craig Stadler, known as the Walrus, winner of the 1982 Masters; and Ben Crenshaw, the immensely popular winner of the 1984 Masters. All three were seeking their first Open title.

Before those three golfers came into view, I saw a cascade of bright red and green and yellow umbrellas and ponchos pouring over the rise in the third fairway—a gallery of several hundred. Then the parade stopped to watch the players' second shots to the green. From my vantage point on the side of a low hill, I still couldn't see the players, but I knew somebody had hit when all the heads swiveled to follow the ball in flight, which I picked up as it sailed toward the green. (It's difficult not to watch a ball in flight, any ball, but sometimes, when I'm standing by the green at a tournament, I'll focus on the empty green instead. Suddenly—thud! Golf ball from outer space.)

The first shot to the third green landed fifty yards short in the left rough. There could be only one explanation for a shot that bad: a bad lie in thick rough. The gallery grapevine quickly verified this hypothesis. Crenshaw's drive had missed the fairway.

Stadler's ball was on the green and Norman's a few feet

short, sitting up on the collar. He could have chipped or putted, so the fans discussed the option and voted for the chip. Norman asked his caddie for the putter. "I don't necessarily agree," one man muttered, and maybe he was right. The putt wasn't on line, and Norman had a sizable par putt remaining. Crenshaw had finally reached the green, though a long way from the hole, with his third shot. As he read his putt, gauging break and slope and speed, the fan who had second-guessed Norman said, "He's got a lot of work here"— standard golf course lingo, usually referring to a chip or a putt for par or worse. You wouldn't say a guy had a lot of work for a birdie, because a birdie is a bonus. Crenshaw missed the putt and tapped in for the bogey with his characteristic gee-whiz frown.

The standard opinion on the tour—pros say it, too, not just sportswriters—is that Ben Crenshaw is more than nice; he's too nice. Truly, there doesn't seem to be a mean-spirited impulse in his makeup. "Gentle Ben" Crenshaw has a minute for anyone and an hour for a lot of people, and that's too much time and energy donated to charity. The pro tour is a debilitating grind of practice, tournament rounds, practice, hotels, restaurants, pro-ams, travel—all of it conducted under the constant pressure of fans, reporters, officials, agents, wives and kids, acquaintances who show up at every stop, and assorted hangers-on. Young pros report that the toughest thing to learn on the pro tour is saying no. Crenshaw still hasn't learned, his friends say, and he agrees, ducking his head with a shy grin. "Yes," he'll explain, "but people have meant so much to me my whole life." That's corny, but it's Crenshaw too.

He grew up in Texas with a natural genius for the game. He was honestly surprised when he missed a 20 footer. The rest of his shots were often wayward, but the putting saved his game. He won everything in college and then his first tournament as a touring pro—in Texas, of course, at the Texas Open in San Antonio—and he finished second the following week. That was 1973. Then nothing for three years. Then victories again in the late seventies. Then nothing again in the early eighties. Then another win in Texas in 1983, and the Masters the following year. But then no victories in '85 or '86 prior to the Open (related in some measure to a recently discovered thyroid problem).

Golfers have been divided into two categories—mechanics and magicians—and the differences in style and temperament implied by that distinction seem pretty valid to me. Crenshaw is a magician. He tinkered with his long, loose swing during the slumps, and once or twice tried to alter it wholesale, but that kind of manipulation requires a tenacity and single-mindedness that just isn't Ben Crenshaw. He finally figured that out and went back to his basic swing and his basic self.

Fans and friends wonder whether he has the killer drive, and he himself wonders. We talked about it one day in Austin, Texas, his hometown, as we rode around and then ate lunch at his favorite chicken-fried-steak place, where old friends from his days at the University of Texas came up throughout the meal to wish him well. I believe the answer to the question is simple. Crenshaw does not have the killer drive. But who says that such an obsession is required? For golfing greatness—Nicklaus greatness—it probably is, but there must be other kinds.

It's axiomatic among golfers that there's no better way to get to know someone than by playing a round of golf with him. That the game reveals character is true up to a point, but if you observe Craig Stadler struggling with a so-so round replete with mutters, tossed clubs, and stalks to the next shot with his head on his chest, you might conclude he's a hard sonofabitch off the course, too. The Walrus is a big, chunky guy built like concrete—hard concrete—and when he spears his 4-iron into the ground, he means it. But in fact, Stadler is one of the more friendly, easygoing, and straightforward of the top players—off the golf course. He's ill-tempered at times, but good-natured.

The game of golf infuriates every kind of personality. One day in northern New Jersey, playing with the regular Brooklyn foursome, I was proceeding along the edge of the eighteenth fairway, minding my own business, when I heard the distinctive and unforgettable *pffttt pffttt pffttt* of a golf club flung head over heels at high velocity past my ear. I watched the club land up ahead, then looked back to see Steve Gaskins empty-handed. Gaskins is one of the most laid-back men I know, but the club went farther than the ball after he topped that fairway wood. I did that once with a 2-iron, which my set is still without because the whirlybird (that's the phrase) struck a tree and snapped the shaft. For years and years the only time I ever saw any sign of temper from my father was when he'd slam the club into the ground and expel a mild curse.

Tommy Bolt and Dave Hill, a couple of old-time pros with famous tempers, espoused this theory: They weren't as good as they thought they should be and hoped to correct the problem by getting mad as hell about it. The classic "angry golfer" photograph shows Bolt hurling his driver into the lake on the eighteenth hole at Cherry Hills, in Denver, in the second round of the U. S. Open in 1960. His drive on the hole had cleared the water—only to hit the far bank and bounce back in. Bad luck on top of bad play was too much.

On the last hole of one of the first televised golf tournaments, back in the sixties, Dave Hill missed a 15 footer, snapped the putter over his knee, and tapped in with what was left. For that he got a big fine and two-month suspension: detrimental to the image of the game. In fact, that tantrum was probably good for the televised game. Golfers enjoy seeing other golfers flame-out.

Club throwing is dangerous anywhere but especially with galleries around, so the tour has tough penalties. I haven't heard about a club-throwing incident in many years. The players don't even spear their clubs very often, a gratifying release of anger I'm sure they miss. A barely controlled toss of the club toward the golf bag—as Bob Eaks did with his putter on the second hole at Shinnecock Hills—is about as far as they can go.

Many good pros had nasty, club-throwing tempers on the course when they were kids, regular little John McEnroes. In fact, some coaches claim to admire that temper, seeing it as evidence of competitive fire. Mainly it's evidence of failure, and then failure to cope with failure. Bobby Jones threw clubs as a kid, behavior he later identified as "puerile." Jack Nicklaus threw a club once, and his father said, "Never again, son, or that's it." And Nicklaus hasn't thrown another club.

My seventeen-year-old nephew, Sam MacNaughton, plays par golf or thereabouts and wants to become a pro. Seven weeks after the Open, I was in Texas to watch him play in the Texas State Junior Championship, held in early August at The Woodlands Country Club in the piney woods north of Houston (Ben Crenshaw won this same tournament when he was fifteen).

The third round was played on a typically broiling summer day in Texas. All the golfers and most of their parents, siblings, and friends were wearing shorts. Sam split the first fairway with his drive, but his second shot on the par-five hole was over the green and unplayable beneath some bushes. I didn't expect him to throw or slam down his club, but I was nevertheless surprised at his phlegmatic acceptance of a penalty on the first hole. He told me later that his stoicism stems in large part from a dressing down he'd received a year earlier from Mike Holder, the golf coach at Oklahoma State University, one of the premier golfing colleges in the country. Holder had known Sam for a couple of years. At a junior tournament in Tulsa, Sam had been tied for the lead until he bogeyed fifteen and sixteen and double-bogeyed seventeen. He slumped off that green with his chin on his chest and then semislammed his golf bag to the ground on the eighteenth tee. Holder saw it happen. "Those are the tools of your trade, son," the coach snapped. "And hold your head up. I don't want to see your head hanging." He told Sam that the fan in the gallery shouldn't be able to tell whether the golfer had birdied or bogeyed, and instructed him to play eighteen as if it were the seventy-second hole at the U. S. Open. My nephew lipped out his birdie putt. He had never been much for throwing clubs; now he doesn't even slam down the bag.

Before the round at The Woodlands I'd greeted him on the practice green, and he didn't look very enthusiastic. His first two rounds were 84-82, way too high; in a practice round earlier in the week he'd shot 72. "Dad's not happy," he said. "I'm just bewildered. You picked the best round to watch. I can't have too many bad shots left."

Sam's father, my brother-in-law, is Jim MacNaughton, a real estate developer who built Quail Valley, a big golfing community near Houston, where Sam grew up with a golf club in his hands. The seventeenth green was his backyard. One of his playing partners in the round I observed at The Woodlands was Brad Montgomery, fifteen years old, whose father, Jack Montgomery, was a touring pro in the late sixties and early seventies. Montgomery is now the club pro at Sugar

Creek outside Houston, about five miles from Quail Valley. His son, too, grew up playing golf.

Jack Montgomery pulled up in a golf cart on the second hole. Brad immediately skimmed two shots. On the sixth hole he pulled his drive and shouted "Thanks!" After the next shot, "Jesus Christ!"

His father watched quietly. "I haven't delivered any ultimatums about temper," he said. "It's a pretty heavy burden to tell a fifteen-year-old boy that if he throws a club—and I know Brad has at times—he won't play again. I try to explain to him that you have to think on a golf course, and you can't think well when you're mad. But if you're going to get mad, at least get it over with quickly."

Sam, meanwhile, was shooting mostly pars with an impassive demeanor, which didn't change when he bogeyed seven and double-bogeyed eight. Nor was there any celebration when he birdied the ninth hole, where he was the only golfer having any success. Brad Montgomery and another member of the foursome lost their composure, tried impossible shots that would have given Ballesteros second thoughts, and threatened to score in double figures. The main reason the pros seldom suffer even a double bogey is that they've learned to cut their losses. They might get angry, but they will not try impossible shots. Kids do. Duffers do. We make the mistake of having a score in mind (a miraculous par, usually) instead of the shot that confronts us. Montgomery watched the debacle on the ninth hole and remarked, "Kids get to running too far ahead, and then they fall behind schedule. Yesterday Brad was ten over par through nine holes. I offered him fifty cents for every fairway he hit, fifty cents for every green, and an extra five dollars if he shot a par 36 for the back nine. I wasn't trying to bribe him. I was trying to get him to think one shot at a time. He missed a 3 footer on eighteen for the 36."

Sam finished the third round with a 77. In his last year of eligibility for the Juniors, my nephew wasn't going to make the cut.

Greg Norman, the third member of that celebrity threesome playing the front nine at Shinnecock Hills, didn't throw clubs as a kid because he didn't play golf. He grew up on a surfboard in Australia and didn't pick up a club until he was sixteen—at least ten years later than most prospective pros have begun swinging at the ball. Norman behaves properly at all times, as befits one of the top five players in the world. (There's some question whether he behaved properly during the third round on Saturday, but that comes later.) Norman looks the part of a hero in all respects, with his shock of white hair, chiseled features, and surfer's build.

Like a growing number of younger pros, he belies the general notion that golfers aren't athletes. That old knock is a compliment, anyway, in my opinion. Golf is an athletic skill, but much more. At the highest level of professional golf, it's not even mainly an athletic feat. Being a great jock might be good enough when it comes to passing or catching or hitting a ball, and certainly when running a race, but Norman's athletic skills alone will never win him the U. S. Open.

I stood beside him one hot, humid afternoon at the 1983 Open in Oakmont, Pennsylvania, while he pounded bucket after bucket of golf balls, working on his driving. This practice followed a round of golf. Sweat poured off his face and soaked his shirt and pants. It is mainly in this respect that golfers must be athletes: Tremendous stamina is required to play the tour.

Tom Watson amazed his new caddie, Bruce Edwards, on their very first day together in 1974. Watson hit practice balls all afternoon on a hot, hot day. Edwards lost count of the number of buckets he fetched. Watson's demonstration of diligence and stamina made a big impression on Edwards, who correctly decided that here was a young player worth sticking with. At Shinnecock Hills, thirteen years and thirty-six victories later, Edwards was still carrying Watson's bag.

Consider the energy required to hit golf balls before a round, work hard for four or five hours during the round, then return to the practice tee for more practice; take into account the demands of intense concentration and the more subtle drain of travel and the constant pressure of people. Pro golf is hard work. Jack Renner, a skinny pro, told me that he was so exhausted one year at The Masters, the last of a long, uninterrupted string of tournaments for him, that he couldn't add up the figures to determine the yardage on his shots (17 yards from me to the sprinkler head, 93 yards from the sprinkler to the front of the green, 11 more from the front to the flagstick, that means I'm . . . I'm . . . how many yards from the hole? The arithmetic eluded him.).

The stamina required for high-level golf isn't the stamina required to lift weights or run ten miles. It's more the energy of a politician running for office, speaking, meeting, traveling, and planning eighteen hours a day, or the energy required of the world-class chess players, who put forth no physical effort at all, yet almost all of whom develop regimens to build up their stamina. A lack of stamina was seen as a factor working against Anatoly Karpov in his marathon championship match with the tougher Gary Kasparov several years ago.

Some politicians don't have the stomach to run for president—that's the phrase used. In fact, they don't have the energy. Without it no one lasts long on the pro golf tour, either.

37

"They'll need every shot in the bag."

"The full repertoire."

"Women and children off the streets."

Two men in their mid-thirties—like most golfers, able to talk a big game—exchanged stock lingo as they analyzed the action at Shinnecock Hills, specifically the seventh green, the masterwork of design they were standing beside. Modeled after a hole at North Berwick in Scotland, the seventh is a par three playing at 188 yards, for the pros only a mid-iron. Looking at the hole from the tee, the elevated green falls radically from right to left. At the crest of the elevation on the right is a little pot bunker; two larger bunkers are installed in the grassy bank that falls steeply away. To the left and short of the green are two more deep bunkers, and the grass surrounding the green is high on all sides.

Basic strategy on the hole: Don't go to the right, from where there is little hope of holding the slippery downhill green with the recovery shot. Left is better, and generally the prevailing southwesterly wind helps the golfer as it sweeps across the green from the right, pushing the ball away from the worst trouble. The best play under usual conditions is a cut shot, a controlled left-to-right fade into both the breeze and the bank of the green. But on Thursday, the Nor'easter blew from left to right, so any shot with the least tendency to go right would go way right. Forget the fade. The opposite shot, a draw into the wind, is today's special. Standing on the tee, all the pros took a little extra time gauging the wind and mulling options they'd already worked out, to some degree, in the practice rounds. This was a dangerous, exciting tee shot.

I watched Kenny Knox, a young player who had won his first tour tournament earlier in the year, do exactly the wrong thing. He let his shot get away to the right and bounce down the grassy slope. Standing on the crest of the hill at the green, he surveyed his situation: Down and to the left was the pin, farther down and to the right was the ball. When he took his stance for the shot, I don't believe he could see the flagstick, but then he did what the pros do all the time. He made a brilliant chip, flipping the ball up and over the rise and just barely onto the green, where it landed softly enough to trickle down to the flagstick, stopping three feet away. The average golfer could stay down the hill and hit that shot forever and not get the ball as close. Knox made par and proceeded to the eighth hole feeling fine, two under for the tournament and, in all likelihood, the leader. I hadn't seen any other red numbers on the scoreboards.

Kenny Knox won a grand total of $26,968 in 1985, placing 146th on the money list. Since only the top 125 players on the list automatically qualify for most of the following year's events, Knox was not assured of playing much tour golf in 1986 or thereafter, until he won in Florida early in the year.

He averaged 72.72 strokes per round in 1985. By comparison, the leading money winner in 1985, Curtis Strange, averaged 71.15 strokes per round, one and a half shots better than Knox—less than a putt per nine holes, a lousy two percent. But that two percent was worth over half a million dollars. No one watching Knox and Strange on any given day could distinguish the leading money winner from the also-ran. Anyone who saw Knox's recovery shot on the seventh green at Shinnecock Hills would correctly assume that he's a fine player. Yet some little difference between his talents and Strange's makes all the difference—at least in 1985. All the pros play par golf, but golf isn't like bowling—par 72 and that's as good as you can get. They have to play *better* than par, they have to shave off the extremely fine difference between a 72 and a 71, between a 69 and a 68. But what is the difference between those rounds? A blade of grass on a green, that's all, or an immeasurably small degree of talent.

At the level of the pro game as it's played on the American, European, and Japanese tours, the differences in skill between the players are almost irrelevant. There are differences—Seve Ballesteros, for one, can pull off shots other pros simply aren't capable of—but the nature of the game tends to even everything out. Par is the great leveler. There are an infinite number of ways to par a hole. Even I can par a bunch of holes in a row. The game will catch up with me, but on one of my good days it might take a while. No wonder, then, that it might take many rounds, many tournaments for it to catch up with a competent professional like Kenny Knox.

At the conclusion of many golf tournaments, half a dozen players are within a couple of shots of the lead, and any of them could have won. The following week, one of them will. While leading the money list in 1985, Curtis Strange won only three of the twenty-five tournaments he entered. He finished in the top ten only four other times. Compare that with pro tennis: Lendl and Becker, Navratilova and Graf proceed straight to the semifinals, and usually the finals, of almost every event. Lendl and Navratilova made almost two million dollars apiece in 1985, almost four times as much as Strange.

The winner of the U.S. Open in golf has to beat 155 excellent players. To earn the tennis title, Lendl and Navratilova have to win seven matches, three of them against unseeded players with almost no chance of winning. Dominance in that sport is easier to enforce. There are no Orville Moodys in pro tennis, no journeymen who come out of nowhere to win the national championship.

Every year on the golf tour, one or two players explode from obscurity only to fall back the following season. They don't disappear, but neither do they regain their brief prominence. No player has been able to establish hegemony since Tom Watson did in the late seventies and early eighties. The leveling nature of the game works against it, as does the growing competitiveness of the many good players who come out of college programs already tournament-tough. This wide-open competition encourages the rank-and-file pros, of course, but worries tour officials, tournament sponsors, and even the players. Everyone understands that fans want heroes, players who win four or five events year in and year out. No one wants a new champion every week.

The tour is not a winning environment. Fine players win just a few tournaments in their careers (Andy North, Peter Jacobsen, and many more), good players might not win at all (Bobby Wadkins). Some of these pros tell reporters, "I'm out here for one reason only—to win. If I wasn't, I'd go home." But they don't win, and they don't go home.

4

⊙　　⊙　　⊙

Once in a great while, inexorable fate loses, or acquires, interest in a particular golfer, and the dogged victim is suddenly and inexplicably its beneficiary.

Consider Andy North, the defending Open champion whose threesome on Thursday morning came to the dangerous seventh hole a couple of groups behind Norman, Stadler, and Crenshaw. North was the first pro golfer I spent much time with. I was working on a newspaper near Houston and his mother worked at the paper, too, and she arranged for me to walk around with her son on one of his practice rounds at The Woodlands, the site of the upcoming Houston Open (the same development but a different course from the one that hosted the State Juniors). That was in 1973, North's first year on tour after a notable all-American career at the University of Florida. He teed off early or I was late to the first tee, or both, and I didn't catch up with him until the third hole, where he greeted me affably. For the rest of that nine we talked about the pro game in the company of his caddie, Russell Steib, a lawyer who prefers golf. (Steib is still caddieing, thirteen years later, but he wasn't employed at Shinnecock Hills. For the last few years he had worked mainly for Peter Thomson, an Australian, on the senior tour.)

North is big and tall, six feet four, two hundred pounds, and at that time, before injuries slowed him down, he hit the ball huge distances. We discussed his golf clubs, the heads of which were loaded down with lead tape. If I hit his high-compression ball with those heavy clubs, he said, it would feel like hitting a large rock with a stick. Force equals mass times acceleration, and I wouldn't be able to accelerate that extra mass of lead. This phenomenon, in reverse, is the theory behind the lightweight clubs, a fad of several years ago: The golfer would compensate for the lighter weight of the clubs with greater acceleration, thereby generating more force. Some did, some didn't, and the clubs failed to catch on. I accepted North's explanation but awaited his invitation to swing the clubs anyway. He never offered, and it probably never occurred to him that I was dumb enough to be hopeful.

In those days, North also struck quite a few crooked shots; too many. His first four years on the tour were winless, then he won a tournament in New York in 1977. The following year he won again—this time the U. S. Open at Cherry Hills. It was my luck that 1978 was the second year that ABC covered the tournament gavel to gavel on Saturday and Sunday—all eighteen holes each day. I followed North's every shot. He led by two strokes after the second round, by one after the third. With only five holes to play on Sunday, he led by four shots, but he gave a couple away and the competition made some birdies. North came to the eighteenth hole needing a bogey to win. Tommy Bolt's driver rests on the bottom of the lake here. North drove safely over the water with an iron, then wisely laid up short of the green with another iron, but in doing so pulled the ball into the left rough. That grass was high, and he punched his wedge shot into a bunker short of the green. I can still hear the dismay in the announcers' voices, especially Dave Marr's. They were watching a man blow the Open, they thought; maybe he already had. (Golf announcers are different from other sportscasters: They openly take sides and root for the players—all the players.)

But North stepped onto the sand and played out beautifully to four feet, directly below the hole. He could sink that putt and win the Open. North putts with his feet wide apart while gripping the putter low on the shaft. Though the stance is not stylish, it was working well that week. North had already holed a couple of long birdies on the eighteenth green in previous rounds. He settled himself over the ball, then stepped back. Oh, he's scared, everyone thought, but North explained later that he was waiting for "a hole in the wind." He found it, settled down again and firmly rapped the putt home. Then he punched both clenched fists in the air.

North didn't win again for seven years, playing poorly most of that time. Injuries nagged him. I saw him off and on, and each time his thoughts were the same: Watching Wisconsin sports was more fun (he works closely with the football team). With each year, it became harder for the golfing press to avoid the conclusion that Andy North was one of those U. S. Open flukes, like Orville Moody in 1969. He resented the insinuation, naturally.

His elbow was operated on in 1983. The following year was miserable, and he earned next to nothing. In 1985 his game began to come together, and in June he won another tournament—the U. S. Open, no less. The dogged victim strikes again.

The site was Oakland Hills, outside Detroit. Half a dozen players had a chance to win, but they all dreamed up ways to lose. Tze-Chung Chen led the tournament by two strokes over North going into Sunday's final round. Then the thin man from Taiwan took an almost unheard-of quadruple-bogey eight on the fifth hole (unheard of for the pros, not uncommon in amateur circles; a snowman, we call it). Even more unheard of was the double hit he perpetrated with his fourth shot on the hole. He hit the ball once where it lay in the heavy grass near

the green, then again in the air on his follow through—
accidentally, of course, as the ball just plopped out of the grass
sans velocity. Chen followed that debacle with three more
bogeys before settling down to finish second by just a stroke.
That was his only top-ten finish in eighteen tournaments in
America.

With seven holes to play, North had fallen two strokes
behind Dave Barr, a little-known player from Canada. But
with six straight pars, North reclaimed the lead and, as he had
at Cherry Hills, came to the final hole needing only a bogey to
win the national championship. That's what he played for;
that's what he made.

Again, I saw all eighteen holes on television. Seven
weeks later, I saw him in Hartford and expressed my congrat-
ulations. He was appreciative, I thought, but cautious.

As far as North is concerned, I'm part of the press—and
following his Open victory in 1978, he wasn't accorded a lot of
respect. He might have thought the second Open championship in 1985 would change all that, but he was wrong.
Questions about his merit didn't go away. Previously the
journalists wrote that he'd won only two tournaments, one of
them the Open; now they noted he'd won only three victories
in thirteen years, two of them *coincidentally* the Open.

North doesn't believe he should have to defend his record. All other modern-day multiple winners of the Open are
acknowledged as great players, including Gene Sarazen, Cary
Middlecoff, Billy Casper, Bobby Jones, Ben Hogan, Julius
Boros, Nicklaus, Trevino, and Hale Irwin. And while North
doesn't insist that he's as great as these players, he does
believe that decent respect is his due. At the pretournament
news conference held at Shinnecock Hills a month before the
Open, the defending champion didn't get it.

"Don't take this personally," the reporter began. "You've

only won three tournaments, but two of them were Opens. What do you say to people who call that a fluke? This isn't my opinion; it's public opinion. I don't mean to insult you."

"But you *are* insulting me," North finally replied. "It's irritating to answer those questions over and over."

He referred the reporter to the scores at Oakland Hills. "Everyone said 280 would be a great score. I shot 279. Five Opens have been played at Oakland Hills and nobody else has shot below par on that course in Open history. If Jack Nicklaus had won, it would've been fine, but some people didn't want me to win."

It will always be fine if Jack Nicklaus wins, and it won't matter if he shoots 279 or 379. Golf fans need celebrities and heroes, and the writers help create them. Writers do, however, need something to work with. North isn't a celebrity or a hero, period, and he doesn't want to be one, and therefore he never will be one—even if he wins a dozen tournaments.

Though writers help create the stars, television is the chief benefactor. Television had the good luck of discovering the game and its market right when Arnold Palmer joined the tour in the late fifties. That was Palmer's luck, too, of course. His bold, dramatic personality and play had always featured boyish grins and stomach-wrenching groans. When he blew the Open at Olympic in 1966 (though, to be fair, Billy Casper played awfully well while catching up), his nine-hole journey of despair was high drama for the "home audience." Arnie's pain ran down the front of our television screens. Everyone else in my family had left for a picnic or something that Sunday when the broadcast opened with Palmer leading by seven shots. I had a hunch to stick around.

Palmer didn't create his dramatics for the sake of his image. He wasn't acting when he scrunched up in despair, or hitched up his pants during a charge, or threw his cap wildly into the stands while pirouetting on the eighteenth green—

the image that made him famous winning the Open for the first and only time, at Cherry Hills in 1960. That exuberance *was* Palmer, and it still is. He came across like gangbusters and made an otherwise tame affair—televised golf—as exciting to watch as Joe Montana at third-and-long.

Nothing has changed. The pros whose personalities make for good television are always the most popular players: Lee Trevino, Greg Norman, Fuzzy Zoeller. That's a short list and I'm not leaving many pros out. The list of players who, like Andy North, don't make the grade in this regard is a lot longer. North's good friend and practice partner Tom Watson was without doubt the greatest player in the game from 1977 to 1984, but he was never idolized by the fans. They acknowledged that Watson was a great golfer even as they still trooped along behind Nicklaus; and if Palmer was playing, they would follow him instead. Watson, a graduate of Stanford with a degree in psychology, is a quiet, undemonstrative player, and he never fully captured the fans' imagination.

Nicklaus is a contradiction to this story, a huge one. His popularity must be laid to his greatness and nothing else. The Golden Bear was booed when he began challenging Palmer, and I didn't like him at all, either. In 1966 a psychologist analyzed why fans booed Nicklaus and came to these conclusions in *Golf Digest:* Nicklaus had the wrong body type (too chunky, almost fat), he was viewed as machinelike and aloof, and he wasn't Arnold Palmer. But then Nicklaus trimmed down, changed his haircut and effectively recast his public image. As Palmer's star waned in the late sixties, the man who had been booed was accepted as the new King of the game. (And then, because *he* wasn't Jack Nicklaus, Tom Watson wasn't revered. Golf fans, it seems, are monotheists.) The fact that Nicklaus was clearly the greatest golfer of his time, perhaps ever, didn't hurt his chances at pulling off that transformation. Now he can weigh whatever he wants to.

His amazing victory in The Masters in 1986 lifted him to a level of acclaim approaching worship. His picture ran on the front page of newspapers all over the country—and elsewhere, I'm sure. People only vaguely acquainted with golf knew that Jack Nicklaus, with a bit of a belly (he feels he plays better at 190 pounds than at a lighter weight) and tears in his eyes and his son Jackie as caddie, had won a great golf tournament at the age of forty-six. You didn't have to be a golfer to appreciate the emotions of that moment. His victory was also testament to the beauties of golf, and it made everyone over forty proud of his participation in the game. Until then merely a hero, Nicklaus was now an icon.

On the Monday before the Open, during the practice rounds, I saw Andy North as he teed off on the fourteenth, a wonderful par four that winds through thickets from a tee on the side of one hill to a green situated at the base of another. The fairway is thin and requires a straight drive. The defending champion's ball sailed way right—in jail, as we say.

Some guy yelled out, "That one's gone!" and didn't seem distraught at the news.

North snapped, but quietly, "Can't fool you." In his own mind, perhaps, Andy North is a dogged victim of more than fate.

The sixteenth hole at Shinnecock Hills is one of two par fives on the layout. Many par fives are birdie probabilities for the pros, who often reach the green in two and have two putts for a birdie; one putt for an eagle is not rare. Sixteen, measuring about 550 yards with a crosswind, was too long to reach in two but, following wedges for the third shot, was still a birdie possibility. A bogey on any par five is just throwing strokes away.

Bob Eaks took an eight on this hole on Thursday—a snowman! His game had indeed collapsed. When I left him after the fourth hole, he was three over and looking shaky. After the triple bogey on sixteen, he was thirteen over par. I watched as the man with the scoreboard posted the green number. Eaks then double bogeyed the finishing hole for a round of 85—fifteen over par. For a professional golfer, even in bad weather, that's embarrassing. Not even a 6–0, 6–0, 6–0 whitewashing in tennis is quite as blatantly bad as an 85. The golfer can't credit the other fellow with great play.

I wasn't surprised when Eaks disappeared immediately after signing his scorecard. However, his playing partners Wayne Smith and Thomas Cleaver were standing around, so I initiated the first postround press conference of the tournament. They were the automatic "leaders in the clubhouse" with their 77s, respectable scores under the conditions. Smith said he was satisfied with his round, and conceded that he'd been nervous over the first putt, the makable birdie attempt, but had then calmed down. I asked him about Bob Eaks's disastrous showing. "Well," Smith replied, "he didn't lose any. But he hit it a lot."

"He hit it a lot." "He got his money's worth." "That was an adventure." Golfers have a dozen phrases to describe the terrible hole, the terrible round. Amateurs take a perverse pride in the fact that their game can be so humiliating. The high score is a badge of honor. Nor are the pros averse to admitting defeat, although Eaks didn't that day. Many times I've heard a pro say, in so many words, "This game humbles you." The immortal Sam Snead once remarked (perhaps apocryphally), after observing one of his pro-am partners hacking at balls on the practice tee, "If that's as good as I could hit, I wouldn't play." Golfers by and large don't look at it that way, and it's a good thing we don't. Otherwise there wouldn't be a game of golf.

Wayne Smith is twenty-five years old, an Australian who plays on the Asian and Australian tours and came to the States solely to qualify for and play in the Open. Qualifying for the tournament was accomplished at a series of preliminaries around the country—quarterfinals and semifinals, in effect. Any golfer, pro or amateur, with a handicap of two or better can enter the first of the two qualifying rounds. The Open is indeed open—if you're good to begin with. (The rules stipulate that a "man's handicap" must be established. Could a woman establish a man's handicap by playing off the men's tees, and enter? It hasn't been tried, and for a good reason. She wouldn't have a prayer in the qualifying tournament, anyway; she couldn't hit the ball far enough.)

It wasn't for want of trying that the Open was Wayne Smith's first professional event in this country. In 1985, he tried to win his playing privileges for the regular pro tour, which is run by the golfers' own organization, the PGA Tour. Qualifying for the tour is almost as difficult as playing on it. Hundreds of quality players try every year: collegians who have used up their NCAA eligibility (some graduate, most don't), players who didn't make it on their first or second or fifth tries, and some former tour players who weren't in the top 125 money winners the previous year and thus have to start all over again.

In 1985, 825 golfers played in eleven regional trials. Smith won his regional. Those competitions reduced the field to the 162 golfers who played in the final qualifying tournament, a six-day, 108-hole marathon in Florida. Fifty golfers placed out of that tournament, but even that showing didn't mean they were on the tour, only that they could line up for places still available for a tournament after the regular tour pros had signed up. Smith wasn't among them. "I played like a blind man in the finals," he said at Shinnecock Hills. So the U. S. Open would be his only tournament in the United States for 1986.

Thomas Cleaver was also playing in his first Open. Twenty-seven years old, having failed several times to qualify for the tour, he played on a small tour in Canada and in minor events in the States. Yet he shot a fine 77 in the horrible weather at Shinnecock Hills.

I returned to the sixteenth green just in time to see Tom Kite miss his birdie putt. He slapped his putter with his hand, and someone in the bleachers beside the green yelled, "Come on, Tom!" Kite glared in the direction of this offending yahoo. Other fans, embarrassed by the implied criticism of the first shout, rescued the situation with shouts of "Next time, Tom" and "Go get 'em, Tom."

Kite is a contemporary of Ben Crenshaw's. Both attended the University of Texas in Austin and live in that city today. They were co-champions of the 1972 NCAA tournament. In personality the two Texans couldn't be more different. Crenshaw is sweet; Kite is sour by comparison. So, anyway, are their public personas interpreted by the press, who are always matching them up. Crenshaw is a dreamer and a magician, Kite a worker and a mechanic. During the 1984 Open at Winged Foot, I was surprised to see Kite practicing on Saturday morning *after* he had missed the 36-hole cut. He stayed in town and worked the whole weekend, then played—and won—in Atlanta the following week.

Crenshaw wouldn't have glared at the heckler, but Kite's somewhat surly reaction expressed the ambivalent attitude many pros feel toward spectators. Some don't suffer the fools gladly. Others don't suffer the fools at all. They acknowledge that crowds go with the territory but dislike the feeling of being owned for four hours by any jerks behind the ropes. Golfers are lucky because decorum has been the rule at golf tournaments—fans walked alongside the players in the fairway until about 1950—but, as a result, they're spoiled. Some are even irritated by encouragement. Many fans have the temerity to believe that they play the same game as the pros, and announce their judgments based on this misunderstanding. "Great shot," someone hollers, and indeed the ball has landed on the green; but the pro, playing his different game, was trying to draw the shot left of the flag, not push it to the right side. So he glares in annoyance. I've heard a fan who wants to know the club selection on a shot ask the player, "Whaddya hit?" and the player respond, "Titleist." That's a brand of ball. That's surly.

After thirteen years on the tour, Tom Kite had won eight tournaments and two and a half million dollars, Ben Crenshaw ten tournaments and two million dollars. Equivalent records, with one caveat: Crenshaw has won a major (The Masters) and Kite hasn't. To be considered a great player today, a pro has to win at least one of the four major tournaments—The Masters, the U. S. Open, the British Open, or the PGA Championship. Nothing else will do, even though many of the most successful pros haven't posted their first major—including Kite, Andy Bean, Calvin Peete, Bruce Lietzke, and Curtis Strange.

Kite led The Masters after three rounds in 1984, but faded on Sunday with a 75. Crenshaw won with a 68. In the '86 Masters, Kite would have tied Nicklaus with a birdie on the final hole. He placed a perfect iron shot fifteen feet from the hole, and rolled his putt across the lip of the cup. The ball could have dropped. It decided not to.

In an interview after that tournament, Kite was asked about the difference between first place and second. He replied, "I don't know that there is a difference. What's the difference between a ball hanging on the lip and one falling in? We'll find out when I win a major if there is something actually different."

That's the viewpoint of a man whose putt did not fall in. Kite, of course, had a good point—what is the difference?—but dozens of pro golfers can rate their own talent against that of more successful players without discerning any appreciable difference. They would admit the difference between their talent and that of Nicklaus, but not between theirs and, say, Kite's; they'd see only that Kite had won more tournaments and more money, just as Kite would see only that Tom Watson, say, had won more tournaments and more money.

Golf is not a game of inches. That's a chasm compared with the tiny distinctions that decide golf tournaments. When the issue of a tournament is settled on the seventy-second hole by one putt that barely catches the hole or doesn't, perhaps critically influenced by a spike mark or a rogue puff of wind or a mere blade of grass, then how important can the outcome be? How important should it be? The only reasonable answer is, Not important at all.

We're silly to invest our egos and energies in such pursuits, but we do. Tom Kite does so as much as anyone, despite his defensive statement after The Masters. He said he'd find out about the difference between first and second *when* he wins a major, but he well knows that he might never win one. And if he doesn't win a major, then—as good a player as Tom Kite is—we'll know once and for all that the spike marks and rogue puffs of wind that are supposed to even out over the course of a tournament, a season, a career, sometimes don't.

At 1:30 P.M. on Thursday, a bona fide blinding storm broke loose from the passing squalls over eastern Long Island, and play was suspended. Rain is one thing, but a driving rain that makes good performance impossible is quite another. Golf is unfair enough as it is. I didn't hear any thunder, which immediately stops play, with or without rain. Since Lee Trevino, Bobby Nichols, and Jerry Heard were struck by ricocheting lightning at a tournament in Chicago in 1975, and hospitalized, golfers have taken no chances. Anyone can walk or run in at the first sound of thunder or the flash of lightning.

USGA officials at Shinnecock Hills, equipped with walkie-talkies, received notice of the suspension and informed the players, who had the option of finishing the hole-in-progress or marking their balls and playing from that point when play resumed. The gusty showers of the morning were assured for the rest of the day, but that afternoon storm seemed of a seaside, ephemeral nature, and indeed the heavy rain moved out and play started again after a fourteen-minute delay. Now it was just windier—gusts up to forty miles an hour and no tall trees to slow them down. I wandered the golf course and therefore missed most of the action. If I'd wanted to see all the shots, I would have repaired to the elaborate media tent and watched on television as ABC fed the video to the ESPN midweek cable coverage. Indeed, beat writers don't spend much time on the golf course. They might get out on one of the practice rounds to study the holes, but during the tournament they watch the shots on TV, listen to the PA announcements, read the press releases, trade anecdotes, and catch the quotes from the leaders who are paraded into the interview room after their rounds. Write it up, and the readers may believe the reporter was everywhere all at once—a miracle of journalism. In fact, he dined well at the buffet and let the tournament come to him.

It's also true that creative directing gives a tournament a

dramatic quality by intercutting players on different holes and pacing it all toward a climax that might as well be fictional. It's a ruse, but an effective and necessary one. No sport is less conducive to television than golf: The action is not in one place, it's not simultaneous, and it's not dramatic. For television's purposes, things couldn't be much worse. A tennis match, certainly, and perhaps even a football, basketball, or baseball game could conceivably make an interesting broadcast with just a single camera or two posted at the correct height and distance. A golf tournament, never. That's why dozens of cameras and the massive logistical backup are called for—to help create a sense of dramatic action where there is none. ABC's broadcast of the U. S. Open is the largest annually scheduled production of the year for any network in any category of show (including the Super Bowl), as rated by hours of air time and people on the job. Yet even bowling can beat golf in the ratings. In 1985 and '86, when ABC had a one-hour bowling tournament matched on Saturday against an hour of CBS's coverage of The Masters, the bowling won. *Bowling!* So how is the Open worth the logistical expense? The audience is the answer, the clearly defined, upscale market that watches golf tournaments. Most of the sponsors are golf ball manufacturers and corporations selling an image— duelling brokerage firms. Other consumer products are secondary, although Cadillac has been one of the two sponsors of The Masters for years. The other is the Travelers.

On television, golf becomes what television producers and most Americans like best, a contest between opponents. The game starts to look like tennis. The actual tournament doesn't have the same feeling at all, and I challenge the honest fan in the gallery to deny that he or she doesn't occasionally, or often, miss the compressed drama provided by television. I know my VCR back home was taping away while I was out at Shinnecock Hills. The coverage of The Masters in April was as exciting a television broadcast as I've ever seen. Place and time magically compressed: Nicklaus, Ballesteros, Norman, and Kite competing in an arena eighteen inches square—the Thrilla in Aprilla, if you will.

So the only reason for the working stiff to drift onto the golf course is to pick up exclusive local color. Here is heralded Scott Verplank playing his first round in his first pro tournament in horrendous purple slacks; Bob Tway, twenty-seven years old, the tall, lanky cover boy, playing with Miller Barber, the fifty-five-year-old dour doughboy whose swing resembles the thrashing of a broken appliance; Jim Thorpe wearing sunglasses on a day when floodlights would have helped; Calvin Peete, a fair-weather golfer, all bundled up in blue and looking miserable.

The leader boards, the few tiny portable TVs, and the grapevine are the only sources of information on the course. A birdie or bogey is posted for a leader and fans start asking, "What happened?" Usually somebody has third- or fourth-hand information. I heard that Tom Watson, three over par at the time, sank a sand shot on eleven from a bunker so deep he couldn't see the flagstick; that's the Watson of old. I heard that Nicklaus lost his ball in the right rough on the tenth hole, and I wish I'd been among the hundreds of Golden Bear fans (a low number due to terrible weather) beating the bushes, dreaming of finding the golf ball and saving Jack Nicklaus a stroke or two. (That would have been an anecdote to last a lifetime. My parents have a minor Nicklaus anecdote of their own. Checking into a small inn in Pinehurst, North Carolina, one of the country's premier golfing meccas, Dad was asked if he wanted the corner room, which was nicer but cost a little more. Go for it, Dad said, and the proprietor informed him that Jack Nicklaus had just checked out of that room after watching one of his sons play in a tournament.)

But nobody found Nicklaus's ball within the allotted five

minutes. It was spotted after he had returned to the tee to drive again. Later, Nicklaus said he probably would've made six from there, anyway.

The practice tee was empty Thursday afternoon. Normally it would have been packed with players working out problems encountered during that day's round, but the weather was just too miserable and the wind too distracting. The pros believe that high winds can damage a sound swing by forcing the player to make subtle, perhaps even unconscious adjustments in an effort to maintain stability. They won't practice in really high winds unless absolutely necessary; unless the swing is so bad it couldn't get any worse.

Officially, seventeen thousand spectators were on the grounds Thursday. I didn't see that many. A lot of fans came and went or settled into one of the hospitality tents set up by corporate sponsors near the practice tee. Bob Eaks had hit the first ball of the tournament at 7:00 A.M. The last threesome was scheduled to take off at 3:42 P.M.: 156 golfers in fifty-two groups. Play was stopped by darkness at 7:53 P.M., however, with eighteen players still on the course, thanks to the rain delay and generally slow play. Those golfers would finish up on the back nine early Friday morning as the regularly scheduled second round got underway on the front nine. Poor play means slow play, and the first four threesomes on Thursday were a combined 121 strokes over par, for an average score of 80. The Eaks-Cleaver-Smith group had been warned on the fourth hole to speed up play—they were three minutes behind schedule. That doesn't sound like much; but if every group falls three minutes behind, the cumulative tardiness jeopardizes the completion of the day's play, and that's what happened on Thursday. Nevertheless, pros resent the timekeepers—unless they're stalled behind some ridiculously slow golfer, of whom there are a few. Nicklaus used to be a very slow player. Former pro John Schroeder had a slow-play reputation, and in 1980 Tom Kite, wired with a microphone for a network broadcast, griped about it on the air. "They should fine him and fine him again." Alas, the remark was taken to say more about Kite than about Schroeder.

Bob Tway led the tournament after the first round with a 70, the only player to match par. He had won the previous week at the Westchester tournament in suburban New York, and twice earlier in the year. This, it seemed, was going to be Tway's year and his twoops were out in force (after Arnie's Army, the headline writers couldn't resist Tway's Twoops. Also, Tway to Go!).

One stroke behind was Greg Norman. Kenny Knox, two under par early in his round, held on and finished tied at 72 with a group including Tom Watson.

Craig Stadler, Tom Kite, Lanny Wadkins, Lee Trevino, and Bernhard Langer had 74s. Ray Floyd, Fuzzy Zoeller, and Seve Ballesteros had 75s. Ben Crenshaw came in at 76. Nicklaus finished with a disappointing but not disastrous 77, tied with Wayne Smith and Thomas Cleaver. Seventy-six players shot 77 or better, and they were alive and well in the tournament. Seven shots behind after one round is nothing, so long as the player improves on Friday.

Defending champion Andy North posted a 79.

5

I had first seen Shinnecock Hills on the Monday before the Open, a bright, sunny day with a stiff breeze blowing from the east, whipping taut the flags atop the poles on either end of the storied Stanford White clubhouse (always "storied," but only indirectly: The famous architect was murdered in 1906 in Madison Square Garden, another of his designs, by one Harry K. Thaw in a dispute over a woman). The long, low, gabled structure at Shinnecock Hills is all weathered shingles and white trim and columns, built along with the first golf holes in 1891 and added onto a couple of times, but not changed much. It's an unpretentious building, and some of the trim needs paint. A sign at the delivery entrance reads TRUCKS KEEP 1 FOOT AWAY OR PAY FOR DAMAGE and, accordingly, a corner there is damaged. The locker room in the eastern end of the clubhouse is nothing but that: wood lockers, a couple of tables and chairs, low-tech showers and wash-basins. The pro shop is a little cabin situated between the clubhouse and the practice ground, and during Open week it was crammed with every imaginable item associated with golf that could bear the stamp of the U. S. Open or Shinnecock Hills or both.

The club bespeaks New England and old money—falsely so, in a way, because the town of Southampton is neither New England nor, any longer, old money. In recent years it has been swamped instead by the largesse of all the investment bankers and enterprising artists who "summer" there. A *New Yorker* cartoon shows a quiet East Hampton street (East Hampton, Westhampton, Bridgehampton, Southampton—all the same thing generically, if not geographically) down which an entrepreneurial type is striding, holding high a fistful of dollars and bellowing, "New money for old!" But Southampton has its ambitions, clearly stated on the little white sign at an intersection near the Shinnecock Indian Reservation: 1640 OLDEST ENGLISH SETTLEMENT IN NEW YORK STATE.

A larger sign greets visitors to Ozona, Texas. BIGGEST LITTLE TOWN IN THE WORLD.

The clubhouse at Shinnecock Hills looks out toward the north from the top of the tallest hill around. The eighteen fairways of the golf course sweep around it in an arc of one hundred eighty degrees. Roughly speaking, the front nine is to the west (or left) and the back nine to the east and straight ahead. Parts of eight holes are seen from that veranda on the hill, including, of course, the eighteenth. An old golf joke has the Scottish visitor asking why every course in America features a downhill first hole and an uphill eighteenth. The answer is that every clubhouse in America is situated on a hill (less common on the links of Scotland), so the first hole leading away from the clubhouse is perforce downhill, and the eighteenth, returning to the clubhouse, necessarily uphill.

Shinnecock is slightly different. Eighteen does return toward the clubhouse, but stops near the base of the hill. Between the eighteenth green and the clubhouse is the ninth green—and so radically uphill from the fairway that it can't be seen by the golfer hitting his second shot. He aims at the top of the flagstick.

All the publicity about Shinnecock Hills boasted of the linkslike land and the return of Open golf to the Scottish roots of the game after decades of championships played mainly on inland courses lined with huge hardwoods. Not quite. Long Island is not links land. It's the moraine of a retreating glacier, as is Cape Cod. And Shinnecock Hills is actually a couple of miles from the ocean, although you can smell salt water in the air. The rough at Shinnecock Hills is unkempt, however, as in Scotland, and the course certainly isn't "treey," as Bernard Darwin, Charles's grandson and the most famous golf writer of his era, phrased it.

On Monday morning, I looked along the line of the first fairway to the west and saw a boat in a bay, Peconic Bay, one of three separating the North and South Forks of eastern Long Island. Beyond the front nine in that same direction rose the landmark windmill of the adjoining National Golf Club, another great layout. Off to the southwest, beyond the practice range and the blue-and-white hospitality tents, was the road and railroad tracks from New York City. A few miles farther away was the Atlantic Ocean, dim in the sea haze. Seagulls circled high overhead and dangling from ABC's big orange crane was the camera platform that would provide the bird's-eye view of the tournament—if the wind died down.

The standard Open or tour layout is green all over, watered everywhere. This golf course was different. The fairways and the greens were vividly green, but the fescues and assorted bushes in the rough and the isolated stands of wind-stunted pines, oaks, locust, and other trees were buff-brown or sepia.

Late Monday afternoon I stood behind the ninth green, then the eighteenth green, and I looked back down those fairways and caught the lingering daylight as the sun fell directly beyond the golf course. The dipping green fairways yawing through the sepia rough reminded me of brush strokes by Morris Louis, or the *Running Fence* that Christo erected across the hills near Carmel, California. Figures walking down the two fairways were small and isolated, as golfers are. The proportions were right.

I like to believe that designer William Flynn knew how beautiful this late afternoon scene would be, but I know better. In the early days, the fairways weren't fully watered, and the irrigation pipes and hoses from a potato-farm system were inadequate without rainfall. In dry spells, the course would have been entirely brown, except for the eighteen greens. Complete irrigation wasn't installed until 1969.

The earliest golf courses on the crumpled Scottish links, the sandy dunes at the mouths of estuaries, date back five hundred years. A couple of these are still in play, and still unirrigated. Nor were those early courses *designed* in the sense we use that word. Golf-course architecture did not begin as such, any more than the visual arts began as *art*. Those early layouts were nothing more than the footprints of the game tracking across the dunes. The flatter places became greens. Certain troughs were less punitive for the player than all the gorse and heather and sand, so these became the fairways, and the traffic over the years permanently defined them as such. The rough was everything else, everywhere else. There were neither strategic nor aesthetic considerations. The land itself took care of those issues.

As golf moved inland and across oceans to less suitable terrain—perhaps less felicitously contoured—the notion of designing developed out of necessity. Only for the past hundred years or so have golf-course architects sculpted the terrain, removed and planted trees, dug ponds and bunkers. The same is true in Scotland. St. Andrews is truly ancient, but most of the other famous courses are relatively new, built or remodeled within the last hundred years. They just look as if they've been in place for eons.

The architects created courses that have now been classified into three main categories: penal, strategic, or heroic. The Scottish links courses are the embodiment of all three. No architect today could propose a manipulation of fairway or green or the devilish placement of a bunker that hasn't been "tried" in its raw state somewhere in Scotland. Some thinker proposed that all of our Western philosophies are a series of footnotes to Plato. Likewise, while today's manicured and pampered New World courses may look very different from their hirsute Scottish ancestors, all design work is really a series of footnotes to St. Andrews, the shrine of the game.

The first designers working in America brought a devotion to the most obvious attribute of the old courses: severity. The penal golf courses designed in this country punish the bad shot. Pine Valley in New Jersey is perhaps the ultimate example. Small targets that suffice as fairways and greens are lost in a vast expanse of sand and scrub and water. Actually, the targets aren't always as small as the impression they give. Bernard Darwin played a round at Pine Valley and had a horrible encounter with the eighth hole. "It is all very well to punish a bad stroke," he wrote, "but the right of eternal punishment should be reserved for a higher tribunal than a Green Committee."

As the game became more popular in the early years of this century, players began demanding a less brutal alternative. Hence strategic design, which emphasizes reward for the good shot and deemphasizes punishment for the bad one—although there's still plenty of that. Here the less-skilled golfer is allowed some hope. In 1933, Bobby Jones teamed with the Scotsman Alister Mackenzie to design and build the most famous strategic golf course in the world, and one of the most beautiful of any kind: Augusta National in Augusta, Georgia, home of The Masters.

"The first purpose of any golf course should be to give

pleasure," Jones wrote, "and that to the greatest number of players . . . because it will offer problems a man may attempt according to his ability. It will never become hopeless for the duffer nor fail to concern and interest the expert."

Indeed, Augusta National is wide open. The fairways are broad and continuous from tee to green, with a couple of exceptions. The rough, except for the stands of pine trees, is minimal. The greens are very large, and there aren't many deep bunkers around them or along the fairways. The holes roll steeply with the terrain and wind through what was a nursery.

I had seen a lot of golf courses, good ones, before I went to The Masters for the first time. It was my luck that rain canceled one of the practice rounds that year and the course was almost empty late in the afternoon as I walked the fairways. No golf course I had ever seen was remotely as beautiful. In fact, no landscape I'd seen was as beautiful. That's outrageous hyperbole, but you wouldn't have to play golf to agree that Augusta National in the right conditions is one of the prettiest spots on earth. The shapes of the greens and the sculpting of the bunkers filled with bright sand and their integration into the broader landscape of fairways and vistas are the equivalent in landscape of one of Henry Moore's heavy, fecund sculptures. Each is a modern art.

Ben Crenshaw, a student of golf-course architecture, pointed out to me another key of the golf course. Unlike many heavily wooded layouts, Augusta National nevertheless feels open. The reason is that among the stands of tall pine trees are large open areas and long vistas. "Too many trees everywhere don't let the eye wander," Crenshaw said. And the eye on a golf course must be given its freedom and scope. That's the whole joy of watching a ball in flight.

Augusta National opened two years after the expanded Shinnecock Hills, which is also strategic in design, but the two courses feel utterly different. When the azaleas bloom in springtime, Augusta is a dazzling jewel box lined with green velvet, open to the sky. Mackenzie wrote that "The chief object of every golf architect or greenkeeper worth his salt is to imitate the beauties of nature so closely as to make his work indistinguishable from nature itself." That sounds good, but there's no question that a human mind and hand were at work fifty years ago in Augusta.

The workmanship at Shinnecock Hills is earthier. The site of the 1986 Open is a jewel in the rough. Playing or simply walking the fairways at Shinnecock Hills evokes the treklike nature of golf, a journey through the wilds.

Golf is the only game in which the fields of play are as highly valued as the greatest players. The golfers come and go while the courses last forever—at least they have so far. They exist in a realm beyond the game itself. The courses don't even need the game. Stretching it a little: A cathedral *is* a prayer. Tennis has Wimbledon and baseball has Fenway Park and Wrigley Field, but golf has scores of sacred sites. Wimbledon and Fenway and Wrigley are structures and, as such, fragile. But the old links at St. Andrews, the newer Shinnecock Hills, even the refined beauty of Augusta National—great golf courses are of the earth.

X

About twenty years after Augusta National and Shinnecock Hills opened, architect Robert Trent Jones (no relation to Bobby) put a label on a design theory that united penal and strategic concepts. The heroic design doesn't require a two-hundred-yard carry over water (as penal would), but it encourages this daring shot by offering great reward on the other side. The less skilled or intrepid player is provided with a safer route around the water. The player who tries the shot and fails will be punished—but he doesn't have to try. That's heroism.

Jones and his contemporaries changed the look of golf courses. The hirsute was definitely out. The new layouts were broad and expansive, a grand scale throughout: tees, fairways, greens, bunkers, and water—lots of water, perfect for heroics. Often the new courses were built on flat land, and lakes were dug to provide the dirt with which to build the greens and give the fairways character. Those courses couldn't exist without giant earth-moving equipment and the sophisticated irrigation and drainage technology required to take care of all the grass. There must be hundreds of them in Florida and the southern tier of states, and now they're found all over the world and are—correctly, I'm afraid—considered distinctively American and modern.

On the ninth green Monday morning at Shinnecock Hills, two USGA officials were working with their Stimpmeter, a simple device that rolls a golf ball down a ramp and onto the putting surface. They chose a relatively level zone; the distance the ball rolled on the grass was measured and recorded—nine or ten or eleven feet—and this figure indicated the relative speed of the green. The goal for Open week was a 10.5 for all eighteen greens. Fast but not ridiculous. In order to achieve that goal, the grass would be cut at five thirty-seconds of an inch.

The condition and speed of the greens are for most pros the main criteria for judging a golf course. They demand smooth putting surfaces with consistent speed. They don't want a fast green followed by a slow one. (On the practice green early in the week, Fuzzy Zoeller would quip, "This green is faster. They're trying to mess us up.") They don't want a green that's fast in the front but slower in the back. They don't want bumpy greens.

Quick greens requiring the purest touch with the putter are mandatory for a major championship (except in the British Open, where the greens are by nature somewhat slower), but the pros justifiably complain when a green is so fast that, in combination with steep undulations, it becomes impossible to stop a putt near the hole or on the putting surface at all, when the merest tap sends the ball all the way to the bottom of the glassy slate, as is the case on some of the greens at Oakmont, a regular Open site, and was the case at Augusta National before they modified two greens that had become ridiculous (even Nicklaus said so). At Shinnecock Hills, the greens were relatively benign and just moderately fast.

Quick greens are just one of the strategies employed by USGA officials to ensure that for this one tournament of the year, if for no other, level par will be a challenge for even the best players. Pros eat up the regular tour stops, where the winning score for 72 holes is ten or fifteen under, sometimes more, and when even-par golf barely covers expenses for the week. In fact, the pros eat up any golf course that isn't specially groomed and toughened, no matter how difficult the design. The odds dictate that in any given week quite a few of them will be on their game, and a hot pro can fire unbelievable scores for a round or two, then shoot plain pars for the victory.

The founding fathers of the Open believe that par, not fifteen under, should be a good score. It is for the amateurs (to say the least), so why not for the pros? Whatever it takes to create this challenge is deemed fair play, including new tees built fifty yards back into the woods, narrower fairways, higher rough. While The Masters is a second-shot and short-game tournament where a hot putter will carry the day, the Open requires more accurate driving, on the grounds that the ability to drive the ball straight is a legitimate demand of the national champion. It's hard to argue with that.

The rough on a basic golf course is cut quite short for average play; a couple of inches or less is considered high enough, allowing the hacker at least to get the clubhead on the ball and advance it toward the green. The rough at the regular tour stops is a couple of inches higher, but at the Open the USGA lets the rough flourish to five or six inches in the areas designated most punitive. In grass that high, the problem is just getting the ball back on the fairway. And the fairways at the Open are narrowed to about thirty yards across, as opposed to the forty-five or more yards in the original design. This "extra" rough, which is nominally irrigated fairway grass, is thicker stuff at three inches than the "real" rough at six inches: It grabs the clubhead with greater tenacity. Therefore, the player who barely misses the narrowed fairway might find his ball in a worse situation than the man farther off line. (And the player way off line, where the gallery has trampled down the rough, might have the best lie of all, but that's an irony beyond USGA control.)

Second-shot accuracy is encouraged by longer grass around the greens, complicating or—in the players' opinion—disallowing the fine art of chipping. If we barely miss the green, they argue, we deserve the chance for a nice chip and putt for par, not this hack-and-hope deal.

The pros complain bitterly about USGA "improvements" that seem to them arbitrary and artificial. At Winged Foot in 1974, winner Hale Irwin staggered onto the last green waving a white towel in surrender. His 287 total was seven over par. At Oakmont in 1983 the players were harsh in their denunciations. Mild-mannered Peter Jacobsen says, "Golf isn't supposed to be played in a bowling alley." Especially not in a bowling alley with the gutters moved in, he might have added. Dave Hill asked, in his book *Teed Off*, "Do they dig chuck holes at the Indianapolis 500?"

The pros point out that the fair number of one-week wonders at the Open—quasi-fluky winners—is proof that the tricked-up courses don't identify the greatest golfers. But the opposite might also be true. The Open identifies the best golfers while the *other* courses merely turn the game into a putting contest. Without question, a certain kind of player does have an advantage at the Open: the cautious, positional golfer who doesn't have to be aggressive on every shot in order to be at his best, who prefers a course on which par is a good score. Nicklaus is such a golfer, certainly. So is Andy North, who at his Shinnecock news conference explained, "It's a different kind of golf than we play every week. It takes experience and patience. A lot of players don't feel they can play under those conditions. I look forward to it." It's not entirely surprising that Lanny Wadkins, perhaps the most hell-bent of all the top players, can't count the national championship among his fifteen titles—though he's had a number of good Opens, including 1985, when he finished just two strokes behind North.

Perhaps the best answer to the issue is Jack Nicklaus's success in the Open—and in The Masters—and in everything else: four U. S. Opens, six Masters, three British, five PGA's, and fifty-two other professional championships (and two U. S. Amateur titles). The greatest golfer wins on all types of courses.

At Shinnecock Hills, the pros were worried about extracurricular matters, too, such as exorbitant hotel room rates and traffic jams—recalling the traffic at Winged Foot two years earlier, when Tom Watson had to lug his golf bag past the stalled traffic and barely made his tee time. Some players catch a severe case of Open-itis the week of the tournament. Nothing suits them. They resent the importance of the whole thing. What makes it so important, anyway? they ask. Bruce Lietzke, a great player with the right kind of game for Open courses, answers that question with his absence.

Except at the four majors, the pros run big-time golf in this country. Payne Stewart, a top young player, spoke for many of his colleagues at Shinnecock Hills: "I would think the USGA would think about the logistics we'll have to deal with. Why in the world take the Open to such a secluded site?"

But the Open championship for men is just one of fourteen national title events run by the United States Golf Association, and only two others are open to professional golfers—the Women's Open and the men's Senior Open. Eleven championships are for amateurs in various categories. Even though the men's Open is the flagship of the line—few fans at Shinnecock Hills could name any of the other reigning USGA champions, including Amateur champion Sam Randolph and Senior champion Miller Barber, who were in the field—and most of the organization's revenues are derived from the tournament, the USGA doesn't pretend to run the show for the sake of Payne Stewart and his buddies. It has loosened up in recent years, now providing courtesy cars for all contestants and a modest buffet in the locker room, but the atmosphere is still much different from the regular tour event, which frankly coddles the players.

The USGA believes that the game is the thing, and the game of golf is essentially an amateur sport, or should be. When Jay Sigel won the Amateur title in 1982, establishment types in the golf world rejoiced. All recent Amateur champions had been collegians waiting to turn professional—semi-pros, in effect—but Sigel was a bona fide amateur, a thirty-seven-year-old insurance man from Pennsylvania who put his clubs away in November and got them out in March. (But

Sigel probably would have turned pro years ago had a hand injury not interrupted his career.)

As it turned out, the pros loved the conditions at Shinnecock Hills, which they declared difficult but fair and refreshingly old-school ("no railroad ties or greens in the middle of lakes," said Jack Renner before he shot an 85 on Thursday and departed). And the traffic was mild, too, thanks to careful planning and the limited number of tickets sold—eighteen thousand per day.

While the USGA officials rolled golf balls down the Stimpmeter onto the ninth green early on Monday morning, a groundskeeper wearing the regulation green coveralls of the Shinnecock Hills crew mowed the adjacent eighteenth green. Gallery marshals drawn from all over Long Island fanned onto the course, wearing spiffy straw hats with red-white-and-blue bands. I lounged in the shadow of the clubhouse, waiting for the pros to arrive for a practice session and a round of golf.

The groundskeeper behind the big power mower was in all likelihood a member of the Shinnecock tribe. Most of the crew of sixteen are Indians, some of them relatives of the employees who plowed the original holes almost a century ago. Peter Smith, the head groundskeeper, is the son of a former head groundskeeper and grandson of one of the original crew. His brother and uncle also work at the club. Smith grew up on the Shinnecock reservation, took a degree in history from Dartmouth College in New Hampshire, decided he didn't like desk work, and returned home.

Other than the crew, few Indians would be around the Open course that week, nor many black people, nor brown. The image of golf as a game for the wealthy and the white is accurate, especially when you limit the focus of inquiry to the game as it's played on the great courses, almost all of which are the de facto segregated playgrounds of the private clubs or the posh new resort courses, where green fees and the (often mandatory) cart fee will run a hundred dollars or more.

Steve Gaskins, the charter member of my Brooklyn foursome who could throw a good fairway wood, now plays at a swank club in Minneapolis, and he almost won his flight in the club championship while wearing sneakers. That showed them. I don't know about his club, but many—hell, most— golf clubs are snobbish places ("snobatoriums" was Rodney Dangerfield's derisive term in *Caddyshack*), extensions of the exclusive residential neighborhoods in which they're located and the executive suites where most of the members work. Dress codes are posted and enforced. Sneakers, well, sneakers don't even *come up.* (The main difference between a *country* club and a *golf* club is that the golf club is more snobbish about the quality of its course and its golfers—no pool or courts, please.)

Golf is Republican country. Tom Watson was close to the mark when he said in 1972 that he was probably the only pro to vote for McGovern. Ronald Reagan won eighty-something percent of the white male vote in the South in 1984, and did at least as well at the country clubs across the land. I don't understand why he doesn't play golf. Eisenhower did little else in his last years. Nixon plays. Gerald Ford is a fixture on the pro-am celebrity circuit and lends his good name to an event held every year near Vail, Colorado.

There wouldn't be many black people in the galleries at Shinnecock Hills, but fewer still, if any at all, on the membership rolls of the club. There's no use asking the board of directors; they don't talk about these things. At any rate, Shinnecock Hills is by reputation an old-money, blue-blooded club. I used to live in Westchester County, which has the largest concentration of great golf clubs in the world—thirty-five in all, fully half of them four- or five-star layouts—and they're either WASP or Jewish, with occasional crossover. Winged Foot, the most famous of them, and host to four U. S. Opens, used to be known as the Irish Y, but now it's Catholic and Wasp, with a few Jewish members. In a piece in *The New York Times* about "signs of change"—a few more Asian families, mainly—one admissions official said, "We are not a discriminatory club, and that's all I will say in response." The question was about black membership, and the answer was ridiculous because clubs are by definition discriminatory. It's no secret that few of the clubs in Westchester have any black members; the only conspicuous exception is Bryant Gumbel of the "Today" show, who plays at Whippoorwill.

With my lackluster capitalist qualifications, I'd have a hard time joining any of these clubs, WASPy as I might be. And without my credentials in the golf world, such as they are, I wouldn't have any chance at all.

The most telling snob story I've heard concerns Cypress Point, the famous postcard on California's Monterey Peninsula. A friend of mine had made arrangements to play the course through the good offices of a member, a well-known figure in the golf world. At the appointed hour, my friend arrived at the clubhouse, found the golf course nearly empty (as so many extraordinary courses usually are) and was told by the man in the pro shop that his tee time was confirmed and he should play right off. My friend, an establishment member of some note himself, said he needed a few minutes to change gear and put on his golf shoes. "May I suggest you use your car," he was told.

John Kennedy played golf, too. Years ago, under some pretext, I journeyed over to the Hyannisport Club to play his layout. The quiet, gray clubhouse sits atop a small hill and looks out over the course, the marsh, and the sea beyond. It was a gray fall day. Waterfowl paraded on the fairways and flew across the sky. Almost alone on the empty course, I didn't pay much attention to the game itself. I was thinking about the first and last politician in this country who meant anything to me, and I imagined him hitting his shots under the careful scrutiny of the Secret Service boys, hampered by his bad back but shooting pretty well nonetheless. He scored in the 80s.

On a similarly gray but rainy day he looked out the window at the White House and imagined fallout descending, too, and he said this testing has got to stop. And it did. He was slow to come around on other issues, including civil rights and a certain police action, but he would have. I know that.

Not all rich, white golfers are Republicans or snobs—I know a number who aren't—and not all good private layouts require a pedigree for admission. The club my parents joined on the west side of Houston is a fairly down-home operation— they chose it for that very reason. And who am I kidding, anyway? I've played with plenty of swells on their exclusive courses—and had a great time in the company of my garrulous caddie. The standard resort milieu is my phobia: huge locker room with color-coordinated carpet and designer sofas, concrete cart paths complete with traffic interchanges and traffic signs, a phony new course—if not a turf nursery (Nicklaus's put-down), just as bad in the opposite direction, an obstacle course—and agonizingly slow play. In short, golf as just another leisure-time activity enjoyed in the stylized, homogenized, and motorized American manner: ride around Pebble Beach for eighteen holes for half a day, then take a drive over to Yosemite. So now who's the snob? I'll admit it, with one caveat: Any golfer would prefer playing on a grand old course with a caddie carrying the bag to driving around the typical new layout.

(I also realize that someone with no money who prefers old money to new money will be without money. It's the munis for me.)

There are 12,346 official golf courses in this country. About forty percent of those are private clubs, forty-five percent "daily fee" (including resorts as famous as Pebble Beach), and fifteen percent are municipal—the munis.

Over four hundred million rounds of golf are played every year. About thirty percent are played on the private courses, forty percent on the daily fee layouts, and thirty percent on the municipals.

The statistics aren't kept, but I don't need them to know that the overwhelming proportion of the golf played in this country by minorities is played on the 1,912 public layouts. The munis are the black and Hispanic "clubs." When I wanted to play on a public course one warm winter day a couple of years ago in Houston, I was urged to go over to Memorial Park. The Hermann Park layout I'd always played before was now predominantly black, I was told. I went over there anyway; it was predominantly black. On just such a muni in Florida one of the top players in the world learned the game. That's Calvin Peete, the most successful black golfer ever, winner of nine tournaments in the last five years (more than *anyone* else), a late bloomer who didn't make it to the tour until his early thirties (he turned forty-three a month after the 1986 Open), a marvel of consistency who hits the ball with a bad left elbow, a crooked left arm and, therefore, a funny-looking swing, but who hits it straight, so straight and accurate the other players are frankly amazed. Peete grew up on a farm with eighteen brothers and sisters and started earning his way as a teenager, selling anything at all to migrant farm workers, following them all the way to the Canadian border as the summer progressed. Only in this peripatetic respect did Peete's youth match that of many of the young pros today, who followed the extensive and growing junior circuit.

Charlie Sifford and Lee Elder and a couple of other black players led the way, and Jim Thorpe is now coming into his own as an excellent player, but Peete has the best record of any black golfer. If he wins a couple of majors, he'll be considered one of the great players in history.

The early black golf pros endured as much abuse as Jackie Robinson did with the Brooklyn Dodgers. Robinson broke into the National League in 1947. Charlie Sifford, six-time winner of the Negro National Open, was the first black man to play steadily on the PGA Tour, joining in 1960, and the first black man to win a Tour event, in Hartford in 1967. No black woman has ever won on the women's Tour. Only a couple have played.

Had Sifford been white, his victory at Hartford would almost certainly have earned him an invitation to The Masters. But he wasn't invited, and no law said he had to be. The Masters is strictly invitational. Sifford won another tournament in 1969, early in the year in Los Angeles, several months prior to The Masters. Still no invitation, and this time Sifford complained openly.

Meanwhile, Lee Trevino, whose first victory was the 1968 U. S. Open, played in The Masters in 1969 but didn't play the next two years. One popular interpretation was that he was boycotting to express his opposition to the discrimination against Sifford; but in a book he wrote later, Trevino said he stayed away only because he didn't like the course. Then, when he returned to Augusta in 1972, he became embroiled in a highly publicized affair about a rejected request for tickets. Nor would he go into the clubhouse, choosing to put his spikes on in the car. A few years later, Clifford Roberts, chairman of the tournament, invited Trevino inside for a cup of coffee. "Just tell Mr. Roberts I don't drink coffee," Trevino snapped.

He now expresses regret about his Masters career, and insists he wasn't boycotting the clubhouse; he just wasn't using it. Perhaps, but after Thursday's dreadful weather at Shinnecock Hills, Trevino said only three tournaments in the world were worth that kind of trouble at his age—the three majors *other than* The Masters. And the following spring brought another dispute between Trevino and Augusta National over tickets. After nearly withdrawing, he played poorly and missed the cut.

In the early seventies, pressure mounted on The Masters to invite a black player. Lee Elder, who hustled golf games on the same muni in Dallas that Trevino had played, won the Nigerian Open in 1971. He thought this victory should have qualified him for an invitation, but received a letter stating that certain foreign championships assured an invitation only to *foreign*-born players.

However, the club did move to protect its flank by establishing clear guidelines to determine who would be invited. If a black man qualified, he was in. All tournament winners on the American tour would henceforth be invited, but there was no grandfather clause, so Sifford couldn't qualify retroactively. He'd have to win again. He didn't, but Lee Elder did, in 1974, and within minutes of signing his scorecard he received a phoned invitation from Roberts. For the rest of that year and the early months of 1975, Elder was widely publicized as the first black golfer invited to play in The Masters. Because of the unparalleled prestige of this tournament, its Deep South setting, and the image of golf as a white man's game, Elder became the Jackie Robinson of the game—almost thirty years after Robinson broke into the major leagues. Elder's first drive in the tournament was right down the middle, but he missed the cut.

Calvin Peete has played in The Masters for years, of course, and the whole subject of a black man playing in the tournament is now dead. Peete goes into the clubhouse at Augusta National, too, but he doesn't see any black members in there. A minor incident at Shinnecock Hills made me wonder how comfortable Peete could possibly feel at the white country clubs that are now his home away from home. On one of the practice days, in the temporary absence of his caddie, Peete was carrying his own bag to the first tee. Already on the tee was Fuzzy Zoeller, horsing around. Zoeller spotted Peete approaching with the bag slung over his shoulder and shouted, "Hey, Cal! Got a loop this week?"

"Loop" is caddie lingo for a job, and most of the black men at pro tournaments are caddies.

I wasn't at that tee, but a pro who was related the episode with chagrin. The playful Zoeller meant nothing offensive by his remark; he might've yelled the same thing at Greg Norman, the whitest, blondest golfer in the world. But if he'd teased Norman, the pro who told me the story would have laughed, perhaps, not gulped.

An episode with flagrantly racial overtones afflicted the U. S. Open held at Shinnecock Hills in 1896. Two young players from the reservation entered the event. One of them, John Shippen, was half black, half Shinnecock, according to the accepted story, but his daughter now insists he was simply black. Some of the participating Scottish and English pros objected to the presence of men of color in the field. Stories vary on what happened next, but almost all versions credit one Theodore A. Havemeyer, sugar magnate and first president of the USGA, with convincing the professionals to play.

Some stories suggest that Havemeyer invented the Indian heritage of one of the local lads, and thus made him acceptable to the visitors. Other versions depict a courageous Havemeyer announcing that the local golfers would play—in a field of two, if necessary. In any event, the Scots and the Brits played.

6

Orin Tucker and his big band played at the grand opening. That's how big a deal it was when the clubhouse and the nine holes of golf at the Ozona Country Club opened in the fall of 1950. Earlier in the year, the Biggest Little Town in the World was the subject of a full-blown profile in *The Saturday Evening Post*, a gently chiding report on the provincial riches of that West Texas oil and ranching center. Some of those rich men were among the eighty-seven founders of the club, and a few of them are active today.

A rancher sold them forty acres at the edge of town for thirty-five dollars per acre. The nine holes were laid out in one day in an arc around the base of a low hill, and the clubhouse was slated for the crook of that arc. The fairways were cleared of mesquite trees and scrub bushes, and the native tabosa grass was allowed to grow in as the fairway turf. The early greens were oiled sand—a common feature of rough-hewn golf courses in those days. A flat rake was used to smooth the line between the golf ball and the hole if it had been tracked up by footprints.

Maybe a half-dozen of that original group of ranchers had ever played golf, but it would be wrong to conclude that the game was as new to West Texas in 1950 as it had been at Shinnecock Hills sixty years earlier. Everyone in Ozona had at least heard about golf, even if they had no idea of how to go about playing it. A pro was hired to sell equipment and give lessons. Until golf shoes were acquired, the men played in cowboy hats and boots and frequently lost their footing on the crumbly caliche soil.

When the greens were converted to grass a few years after the course opened, a simple watering system was installed to service them. In 1963 the course was radically upgraded with bermuda grass fairways, bent grass greens, and an expanded fairway watering system. In 1971 an automatic PVC irrigation system was added—only two years after Shinnecock Hills was so equipped. Throughout those two decades of improvements, members did most of the work. Today, the Ozona Country Club is the best nine-holer in the country (meaning the general area; within several hundred miles in any direction). All West Texas golfers agree on this. You have to drive almost two hundred miles to the east, to San Saba, the pecan capital of the world, to find a better nine holes of golf.

The biggest town of any size near Ozona is San Angelo, eighty-five miles to the northeast, population 75,000. A little farther away and to the northwest is the Midland-Odessa metroplex, population 160,000—and falling, but not as quickly as the price of oil throughout most of 1986. About the same distance to the west is Fort Stockton; to the south, Del Rio on the Mexican border. Two cities most people have heard of are San Antonio, two-hundred-plus miles to the east on Interstate 10, and El Paso, somewhat farther to the west.

A metropolitan population of fifteen million lives within one hundred miles of Shinnecock Hills. One hundred miles from Ozona in any direction is mostly vacant territory—as true now as in 1950. This part of Texas is called the Permian Basin, drawing its name from the Permian period, the sixth and last period of the Paleozoic era, about 250 million years ago, during which a "marine submergence" held sway over

Ozona and environs, laying down deposits of marine lime-
stone and sandstone thousands of feet thick. They're still
there, along with the Ogallala Aquifer, the massive subterra-
nean river that services a ten-state region stretching north
almost to Canada, and the Edwards Aquifer, which irrigates
the Ozona Country Club. In a way, oil and water can mix.

The town of Ozona was founded in 1891, the same year as
the Shinnecock Hills Golf Club. A dozen or so West Texas
homesteaders acquired the land for a dollar an acre, or leased
it for pennies from the holders of the original land grants, who
were mainly the railroads, the University of Texas, and other
public entities. Crockett County alone, of which Ozona is the
county seat, has 1,788,000 acres of pasturage, almost three
times the area of Rhode Island. The ranchers had up to forty
years to pay it all off, plenty of leeway.

"Despite periodic droughts and occasional whistling
northers, the high dry plains around Ozona have produced
great riches in the form of wool and mutton, mohair and oil,
and no citizen fortunate enough to have been born in Crockett
County has ever felt any deep urge to quit his ranchlands or
abandon his spacious residence at the county seat even to
savor celestial joy beyond the pearly gates." Those spacious
residences referred to in *The Saturday Evening Post* story are
one of the more incredible sights in West Texas, in my opinion. Other travelers would dispute this, arguing that there are
no interesting sights at all. This is the country where *Giant*
was filmed—to be exact, on the Evans ranch in Marfa, farther
west—and which so appalled Leslie Benedict (Elizabeth Tay-
lor) when she arrived from the wooded hills of Virginia and
first saw Bic Benedict's (Rock Hudson's) barren Reata ranch.
Before Interstate 10 bypassed Ozona proper, the only east-
west route through Texas from Houston to El Paso was the
main street in town, and the weary motorist was suddenly
confronted with the incongruity of a dozen handsome man-

sions, side by side, lawn-surrounded, tree-shrouded. There might not be any other pecan, oak, and magnolia trees this tall within one hundred miles.

In 1950, Ozona was home to about thirty-five hundred people. Today that number has swelled to about four thousand, including four generations of the original ranching families. At the height of the oil boom in the early 1980s, Ozona had a population of some five thousand. The fact that a fifth of the boom-time citizenry left town so quickly with the oil collapse proved to my grandmother that she was correct in her assessment of the civic commitment of those oil-field workers and their confederates. She had been suspicious of their mobile homes all along. The country club membership of three hundred fifty has held up well during the exodus.

My grandparents moved to Ozona in 1957 from Stamford, where I was born, two hundred miles to the north. The change from the farm land up there to the pasture land of Crockett County didn't affect my grandfather. He was the local hospital administrator in each locale. I spent many weeks of my summers in Ozona as the visiting grandson of Bailey and Myrtle Post. My granddad wasn't one of the wealthy ranchers, but given his position at the hospital he knew just about everyone in town, including many of the Mexicans (who were, and are, about half the population). I rode around town with my grandfather in his black Chevrolet as he collected the mail, negotiated with the butcher, and picked up the blood at the bus station. Almost everyone we passed at our slow speed greeted Bailey Post, and he returned this greeting with a vertical movement of one finger of the hand that rested on the steering wheel. Occasionally my older brother and I were invited to a party at one of the ranches and we went, although I, for one, preferred to hang around the house or the hospital with my grandparents. I was glad they'd moved down from Stamford, where my father's parents lived and my other granddad sold Studebakers and ran the cotton gin. Two towns to visit were better than one.

Bailey Post had an ancient set of left-handed golf clubs, and he might have used them out at the country club, which is right across the San Angelo highway from the hospital. No one recalls. Although not a member, he would have been welcome.

In September, three months after the Open at Shinnecock Hills, flying from New York City to Ozona via Midland-Odessa, I was surprised to learn that there was regular jet service between Dallas–Fort Worth and Midland-Odessa. But that only shows that I haven't spent much time in Texas since the oil crises started driving up the price of crude beginning in the early seventies. Then the price had plummeted, but the flights remained on a limited basis. The stories I'd heard in New York painted a bleak picture of Midland-Odessa withering away in the aftermath of the crunch, but Dick Webster, my contact man in Ozona, assured me that a good number of golfers from up there would still be going down to the Invitational.

I rented a compact car at the airport and headed east to pick up the road to Rankin—south to Rankin, east to Big Lake, and southeast to Ozona. The big news at the airport was the heavy rains and flooding in West Texas, and that worried me. The Invitational began the next day. If the course had flooded recently, it might not be playable, although it might've been just fine in this dry land (average rainfall: eighteen inches) where water runs off quickly. I stopped at a truck stop to get coffee and call ahead.

Dick Webster wasn't at the Flying W Motel, which he managed with his wife Mary, but Mary reported that Ozona had been spared: plenty of rain in the preceding month but none in the last few days, and no floods. Rain was forecast, but the tournament was still scheduled. As I headed out, the waitress urged me to come back when I had more time. Texas hospitality.

Showers were in the area, all right. On the road to Rankin a wide section of sky to the east was black from the horizon to straight overhead, while right in front of me were bright shafts of light. I needed my sunglasses as the fat sprinkles at the edge of the storm struck the car. A West Texas thunderstorm can drop many inches of rain in less than an hour, and this one was well on the way. A local deluge has distant repercussions as flash floods race through shallow gullies of towns that haven't seen rainfall in a month: gully washers.

I caught the edge of one last deluge outside Big Lake, a depot for the oil field. On the Ozona side of Big Lake is a low, flat spread of land that was dry as a bone despite all the rain around. A large sign posted in the middle asked, WHO PULLED THE PLUG ON BIG LAKE?

Regarding the body of water, no one. It dried up spontaneously years ago, and the water hasn't returned. Regarding the depressed economy of the town, some combination of the big oil corporations and the Arabs is the general opinion.

The grasses all the way from Midland-Odessa were green and fresh—not the rich green of a wet climate or the lawns of Ozona, but the olive green of the native tabosa. The land was beautiful. The storms were apocalyptic. I was delighted to be going home. And Friday was a cool day for early September in Texas, when ninety degrees or higher is as likely as anything. Instead, it was seventy-five and partly cloudy, the air as clean as I remembered from years before when granddad and I used to sleep on the screen porch, where sleeping doesn't get any better. Ozona is three thousand feet high, and it was named for the rich smell of the ozone that sweeps down from the stratosphere, or wherever, during thunderstorms.

When I visited West Texas regularly, twenty-five or thirty years ago, motorists on the highways almost always acknowledged each other with a tip of the hand. It was expected. Driving down to the Ozona Invitational, I decided the tradition had lost some of its imperative. A number of cars passed me without a sign. Then an old codger lifted his hand and I was so surprised I didn't have time to return the greeting. But I remembered how it was, and I started watching. I took the initiative myself several times, with mixed results. It's mostly the truck and pickup drivers who still indulge.

The country club in Ozona is just north of town, banked against the small hill, the white clubhouse and olive-green fairways visible from the highway. I drove past and headed into town to check in with my grandmother, who lived in an apartment on the western edge (and who now lives in the nursing home next to the hospital). She was eighty-nine years old when I visited; my grandfather died in 1979, when he was eighty-three. Myrtle knew I was coming down to write about this local golf tournament, but she was under the impression that some of the great pros were competing, and she had read through her latest issue of *Golf Magazine*, looking for a reference to the Ozona event. Why else would I be there? she wondered.

I asked her if she'd ever played golf. She answered with such a harsh No! that I thought she was denouncing the very idea, much as she had another one years ago when I kiddingly wondered if she had ever seen an issue of *Playboy*. Knowing that she was embarrassed by the soap operas, I was mildly surprised that she'd even heard of the magazine. Her game is baseball.

After settling in with her, I set out to find Dick Webster at the Flying W, a mile and a half on the other side of town, beyond the row of stately mansions and, at the end of the row, the Methodist Church. Mary Webster said her husband was out at the club.

In the parking lot, my compact car was the only one around. Everything else was a pickup or a large sedan or family van. Nothing Japanese, nothing German, all American. Over the weekend I saw only one foreign car, an Audi.

The clubhouse of the Ozona Country Club is a single-story building with offices, kitchen, ballroom, card room, and the bar. Conspicuously absent is the traditional locker room and showers, because no one wants either one. Members use their golf cart sheds as lockers, and they shower at home.

On one side of the clubhouse is a small, covered patio with a take-out window connecting it to the bar inside. That patio was where I found Dick Webster and a dozen other golfers on Friday afternoon, drinking beer. Webster introduced me as the journalist from New York in town to cover the Invitational. This announcement was greeted with puzzlement, perhaps even suspicion, until Webster added that I was almost a local boy . . . in a way . . . a long time ago. And everyone knew or knew of Mrs. Post. Now my presence made more sense.

But exactly why was I writing about golf in Ozona? I explained about Shinnecock Hills on the one hand, Ozona on the other. "The high and the low!" someone interjected, and I begged to differ. Before I knew how it happened, I was a member of the club and therefore legally eligible to drink a beer; I chose Lone Star. Crockett County is dry—no retail sale of liquor is allowed. (The Methodists claim the Baptists vote "dry" and the Baptists don't deny it, nor do they deny that they drink liquor.) Private clubs in the dry counties in Texas can serve alcohol, so any restaurant desiring to do so designates one room as the "club," and you join on the spot.

On the patio I met Horses and Mustard Williams, two of

the founding members, and two of the five Williams brothers in town. The other three are Skineye, Sec, and Huista, and there is, of course, a story behind every nickname. Horses was the only one playing in the Invitational. Mustard plays golf but not in tournaments, and Huista had a broken collarbone; the other two brothers don't play at all. On Saturday night Mustard would be handling the Calcutta auction—a technically illegal gambling enterprise—as he had for years.

The Williams brothers were born, bred, and still live in Ozona, where they ranch and do other things. *The Saturday Evening Post* reported that few Ozonians feel any reason to leave. Of those who do, few go far. I met David and Mike Williams, Huista's sons and low-handicap entrants in the Invitational. David, a land man in the oil business, now lives in Midland. A land man is a real estate agent, in effect, who puts together leases, but Williams hadn't worked in the field for six months, and he might not work again until the price of West Texas Intermediate goes up to twenty dollars a barrel. In early September it was selling at sixteen dollars. He was unhappy about the situation, but it gave him plenty of time to play golf, and he had a 6 handicap to prove it. "I want to play St. Andrews," he said to me urgently.

Mike works in the oil field construction business, and times were hard for him, too. He has a 3 or 4 handicap. The two brothers played golf every day in Austin when they attended the University of Texas. Playing on their team in the Invitational would be Mark Harvey, a contractor in Houston who also played golf every day in Austin. Harvey was planning to drive eight hours on Saturday to make the 1:30 tee time, then he'd drive back home Sunday evening. (Long distances are no obstacle in Texas, where you wouldn't think twice about driving one hundred miles for barbecue and beer, much less five hundred to play golf.)

The fourth member of that team was Duane Childress, a

young rancher with a famous ranching name. He wasn't
around on Friday afternoon, but his father was, and that
wasn't surprising because the golfers in attendance agreed
that Pleas Childress plays more rounds at the Ozona Country
Club than anyone. "I play almost every day," Childress *père*
acknowledged.

Filled with more facts and faces and names than I had a
prayer of remembering, I walked onto the Ozona golf course.
The nine holes wrap around the clubhouse and the hill (it's a
very low hill) in a double loop, and play proceeds out and back
one loop (the first five holes), then out and back the other.
Play the course twice for eighteen holes: par 36-36—72 for the
Invitational.

It's a basic golf course, even more basic than the Texaco
Country Club—no sand bunkers greenside or fairway, only a
few grass bunkers or barriers. The only water is in the concrete tank on the ninth hole, way off to the right but in play
often enough. Winter rules apply at all times, as specified by
local rule number 7 on the scorecard. The ball in the fairway
may be "rolled over" with the clubhead to improve the lie, but
no nearer the green. Winter rules are often invoked on
courses that have spotty fairway grass. "Not enough fodder,"
Horses Williams said with a grin, but the Ozona fairways
looked pretty good to me. I've played on a lot worse, and I
know the West Texans have.

Because the layout loops in a counterclockwise direction,
eight of the nine holes are out-of-bounds to the right, and the
fence line is at the edge of the fairway on the second, third,
fourth, sixth, and seventh holes. Thus the amateur's favorite
mistake, the slice, is disastrous on this layout. The better
player's mistake, the hook, will never be out of bounds, but

St. Andrews is laid out in the same fashion, out-of-bounds to the right most of the way around. And besides, golf isn't supposed to be fair.

The fairways at Ozona are as wide as the rough is hazardous: bare caliche soil, scrub bushes, rocks, live oaks, and mesquite trees. The greens are tiny—and that makes all the difference, despite the absence of bunkers. They were in fairly good shape in September, although uneven in their play. The ball might bounce hard in front of the green on one hole, and almost plug on another. That makes running an approach shot onto the green a dicey prospect, and the pros would object, but to heck with them.

The layout has a pleasant feeling, and this intangible is an important factor when golfers judge a layout. I think it comes down to this: Does a golf course feel as if it *belongs?* From any point on the Ozona nine, the golfer can see the play on much of the rest of the course. Isn't this as it should be in a land of long distances, where motorists gesture in passing—or used to? In West Texas, a course with hardwood-lined fairways, lakes filled with blue-dyed water, and bunkers with white sand shipped in from Florida would be silly. A fancy layout in West Texas that didn't leave a lot of room for the sky and the horizon would look lost on this contrary landscape.

My tour of the layout completed and most of the golfers gone home, I joined Horses Williams, his wife Jonesy, and my grandmother for Mexican food on the other side of the interstate. Jonesy was the head nurse at the hospital during Bailey Post's tenure and she essentially takes care of Myrtle today.

A few of the other diners greeted our group as we threaded through the tables, and that reminded me of the story my nephew Bobby relates about his visits to Ozona as the great-grandson of the Posts. When my grandmother took him and his sister Nicole into a restaurant, the men at the tables wouldn't exactly rise as the Post party proceeded past, they'd just lift slightly in their seats, tip their cowboy hats, and intone, "'lo, Ms. Post." The *Ms.* had nothing to do with feminism, either; just another contraction.

The Williamses are active members of the West Texas–New Mexico Seniors Golf Association, and they travel all over those two states and as far as California to play. The group has four hundred members and sponsors two major tournaments every year. Seniors' golf is what the game is coming to. According to the surveys of the National Golf Foundation, almost half of the "avid" golfers in the country (twenty-five or more rounds per year) are over fifty years old. I don't like golf carts, and I tend to disdain the golf courses made for them, crisscrossed with asphalt or concrete paths, but that's not a fair attitude. The carts do make it possible for many older people to play the game, certainly in the hot weather in Texas, and it would be perverse to argue that golf courses should be protected from mechanization for the same environmental reasons that obtain to national parks. I recall the first time I saw my father riding in a golf cart—an awakening equal to my realization that his hair had turned gray.

Horses Williams started playing golf when the club in Ozona opened. Jonesy Williams got a later start; she didn't have the time when she worked at the hospital. She told me her most recent round was 105, with 38 putts, and I gathered that 38 was better than her usual work on the greens. Many women play golf at the Ozona Country Club, although none would be playing in the Invitational. That's a men-only affair; women have their own big tournament, with about the same number of golfers coming from all around. In a way, the separate men's and women's tournaments are anachronistic, as mixed-team golf has become the major trend in the game, certainly for seniors.

Women play a different game from men. Few women hit the ball with power. My mother cannot hook or slice the ball to any damaging degree—she doesn't hit it hard enough to impart that much spin. She hits it straight—not far, but straight. The tees for women are set forward of the men's tees as much as fifty yards, maybe even more (with the regular men's tees a corresponding distance in front of the championship tees), and this yardage compensation is supposed to make up for the difference in strength. The women's game is closer to mine and the average amateur's than mine is to the pros'. The amateur might be advised to take lessons from a woman instructor, but from what I've seen, most of them wouldn't do it. (On the women's pro circuit a funny phenomenon is the pro-am machismo, when some of the male amateurs feel obliged to outdrive the pro or pull a muscle trying.)

Horses Williams looks out on the flat world of West Texas with a squint and a grin and an unlit cigar clamped in his jaws at all times (he put away the matches after he almost died from a hemorrhaging ulcer a few years ago). He and John Childress—one of the ranching Childresses, of course—have been partners in twenty-two different businesses in the past three decades, including ranching, oil and gas, a feed store, an auto dealership, and a motel or two. Few of the ranchers in Ozona just ranch. When the oil prices soared in the seventies, the free money floating around had to be spent. The most notorious example in that part of the state is the Circle Bar Truck Corral, seven miles east of Ozona on Interstate 10. Tom Mitchell, a nongolfer, built that Taj Mahal of truck stops, which has every amenity including a lush indoor swimming pool and garden.

Horses's theory is that the Arabs and the "majors" are conspiring to run the independents out of the oil business; as soon as this goal is accomplished and the small fry (including some very large West Texas ranchers) are gone, the cabal will jack the price back up to sixty dollars. This theory is not Horses's alone. Ranchers have seen wild fluctuations in the price of other commodities, and their feeling tends to be that if the weather isn't responsible, some kind of chicanery must be. The oil patch in Texas has watched the price of West Texas Intermediate in the last two decades soar from four dollars to over thirty dollars, then plunge back to six or seven. Now it's going up again, but slowly.

Somebody is sandbagging. In golf, that's when you manipulate your handicap for competitive advantage.

The sun was just coming up on Saturday morning as I drove to the cafe at the Inn of the West to join some of the golfers for coffee. In Houston, in New York City, in Westchester County, or on eastern Long Island—there's no equivalent in these places to the transparently blue sky of the early morning in West Texas. A few showers had dampened the ground overnight, but the morning was warm and clear. The *San Angelo Standard Times* on sale in the motel lobby celebrated the rainfall with the traditional red rooster. I remember when the rooster was superimposed over the entire front page. Now it's just an emblem at the top, but weather will always be front-page news in West Texas, and not because it might affect the Ozona Invitational.

The price of gold was the subject around one side of the table. The price of anything would elicit interest in Ozona, a thoroughly mercantile civilization. The main story in the newspaper wasn't mentioned by any of the golfers at the crowded table—dateline India: "17 Dead in Plane Shootout." If it had been, the conversation might have shifted to the Indians or the Pakistanis—no one seems certain which—who own the Silver Spur, another motel in town. Agents of these Asians bought up many motels in West Texas during the oil boom, but their enterprise is not looked on kindly in Ozona, I gathered. There's a theory in Texas that West Texans are more friendly than East Texans because of the openness of the western terrain compared with the thickly wooded land in the eastern half that supposedly induces paranoia. I've lived all over the state and dispute the theory. The key to this issue is the size of the town, and that's not just in Texas. As I was introduced around the table as the fellow from New York who used to visit his grandparents in Ozona and was now back to write about the golf tournament, someone remarked, "You can be born here and still be a Yankee!"

As the group started to disperse for the course, "the numbers" were picked to determine who paid for the coffee. The numbers is the traditional manner of paying the coffee portion of the bill in Ozona when a large group gathers in a cafe, as it often does. Most of the people know most of the other people and are related by blood or marriage to a good many of them. (At the club the previous evening someone said, "I learned long ago not to talk about anyone around here.")

Nick Nicholas "won" the numbers game—I didn't understand the quick explanation—and picked up the bill. I paid for my own grits.

The entry fee for the Ozona Invitational was $150 per team, which bought liquor and barbecue at the party Saturday evening and a crack at the cash prizes for each of the four flights:

$500	WINNER
$350	SECOND PLACE
$250	THIRD PLACE
$100	FOURTH PLACE

In amateur tournaments the golfers are flighted according to their handicaps, and a separate competition is played within each flight. At some tournaments the first day's play is in effect a qualifying round, and the flights are then established on the basis of the first day's scores. The danger here is sandbagging, whereby an artificially high score is recorded (it's easy to miss a few putts) in order to establish a handicap higher than it should be. The sandbagger would then have an advantage in his flight when he played to his real ability the following day. One way to circumvent sandbagging is with preflighting, the format adopted in Ozona. The disadvantage of preflighting is that a team could have been sandbagging for a whole season, or simply have reported bogus handicaps on their entry form. But no handicapping system is perfect, and the Ozona organizers know most of the golfers anyway.

Another potential problem in amateur golf is the inequity almost inherent with handicaps: a 15 handicap established at Shinnecock Hills would signify a different quality of golf from that same handicap earned at the Ozona Country Club, where it's easier to post lower scores, presumably, because Ozona is an easier golf course. The new Slope system devised by the USGA addresses this problem by including a rating for course difficulty in the computation of handicaps. The Slope rating for Shinnecock Hills is 71.6 from the championship tees, 67 from the regular. Ozona hasn't been rated yet.

In any event, the handicap of the golfers within each flight at the Ozona Invitational broke down this way:

CHAMPIONSHIP: 0–6
FIRST: 7–10
SECOND: 11–15
THIRD: 16 and higher

Within each flight, the competition would be played at stroke, without regard to handicaps. A team's score for a hole would be the sum of the two lowest scores in the foursome, discarding the two highest scores. In fact, if one player was out of a hole in terms of helping his team, he'd put his ball in his pocket to speed up play. Some tournaments sell one mulligan for each round. A mulligan is a second chance, and it makes for an interesting game: after which bad shot should I use it? Other tournaments allow one free kick, presumably from behind a tree. But Ozona plays it straight.

In most instances the four players on a team were of the same caliber. A notable exception was Dick Webster's team, in which Webster, an average player, joined three other very good players—including his son, Rick, one of the best golfers in the tournament. With a fourth strong player, that team would have been in the championship flight. As it was, they'd look good in the first flight.

Eighteen foursomes would play in the morning and eighteen more in the afternoon. For Saturday's first round, foursomes from each of the four flights played in the morning and the afternoon. For Sunday's second and last round, the championship and first flight teams would play in the afternoon—a break for the better golfers, most of whom, in West Texas, don't like to play early. In Ozona, the traditional time for a round of golf is 1:30. Anyone intending to play gathers on the first tee, matches are made, and play proceeds twice around the course and thence into the air-conditioned club. In Houston, by contrast, where it's perhaps less hot but certainly more humid than Ozona, players vie for the earliest possible tee times and the courses thin out in the afternoon.

The parking area in front of the clubhouse and next to the first tee was already jammed with pickups, sedans, and golf carts when I arrived. Golf carts everywhere. Some golfers might double up for the tournament, but in other foursomes each golfer would ride in a separate cart. In West Texas, golf and carts have always been inseparable. The cart and the electricity it burns are part of the start-up cost when you take up the game. In Ozona, four long rows of sheds house the carts, one hundred forty in all, and the club assesses each one sixty dollars per year for charging the batteries. Visiting players either make arrangements for a local cart whose owner isn't playing, or they bring their own.

The players traveling the farthest, from Lamesa, fifty-five miles north of Midland, pulled up towing their two carts on a flatbed trailer. That group, one of the favorites in the championship flight, was led by Butch Gerber, former coach of the Ozona High School golf team, and starred Jess Claiborne, Southwest Conference champion for Texas Christian University in 1968. Claiborne told me that he grew up riding a series of Cushman scooters, chopped off English Fords, and any other kind of motorized transportation available. "Walking on a golf course in West Texas," he said, "is like being on an interstate with your back to the traffic."

West Texans are aware that the game wasn't founded on this motorized principle, and they know that on the traditional Scottish links there are virtually no carts, but they also know that it's hotter in Texas than in Scotland, and they know the way they like to play. Besides, you need a cart to carry an ice cooler. The model Dick Webster outfitted me with was an old-fashioned three-wheeler, excellent for quick cornering.

The Invitational was scheduled to get underway at 8:30 with a shotgun start: two foursomes on every tee, play beginning simultaneously on every hole. That's the way to pack a golf course and get a lot of golfers around in a hurry. The pistol fired at 8:32 A.M. On the first tee a supervisor for the Texas Department of Public Safety named I. V. Babbitt, a tall man wearing shorts and sneakers, leaned over his golf ball with legs spread wide like a giraffe going down for water and swung quickly. The ball veered down the right side of the first fairway—a slice. The first hole at Ozona is a dogleg left, and that spelled trouble for Babbitt's slice to the right, but the fairway is wide and he thought his shot had caught the right edge of the short grass, just beyond a rise that hid the landing area from the tee. His teammates assured him that this was the case. Babbitt stepped back and grinned: He had gotten away with a slice, the shot that had bedeviled him for years, until he discovered the trick of the spread-out legs.

That was a new one on me. I've always countered a slice or a fade early in a round of golf by taking a few practice swings with the feet absolutely *together,* thus promoting a full turn of the shoulders and spine and setting up the preferable inside-out swing that should draw the ball. I thought Babbitt's contradictory solution would aggravate his slice, not cure it, but I was wrong.

Next man up for the Department of Public Safety team was Randy Hall, a dispatcher, my grandmother's former neighbor at the apartment house, and a man whose golf swing I had already been told about. Indeed, I've never see another like it. Hall swings twice. Diligent fans of pro golf will recall that Arnold Palmer some years ago developed an unusual putting stroke, drawing the clubhead back in what appeared to be the real stroke, bringing it forward in what appeared to be the real stroke—but stopping short of the ball. *Then* he made the actual stroke. Though the aborted stroke wasn't a yip, it's hard to understand how it was designed to help Arnie sink putts. Randy Hall does exactly the same thing with all his shots: a full swing aborted at the last moment, then the real swing—and the ball goes straight down the middle. Thus Hall's sporty 6 handicap.

Hall is a cheerful fellow, so I hazarded the obvious quip that someday he'd turn in a 75 and an official would say, "No way, Hall. That's 150." Hall just smiled, and I believe he'd heard that joke before. He said he got the double-swing habit from the practice swings he took playing softball, the other

main summertime activity in Ozona, so it just seemed natural
when he began playing golf. A rule I've established over the
years decrees that whatever seems natural in a golf swing is
probably a mistake, but Hall contradicts it.

As the four members of the DPS team hit their drives on
the first tee, Dick Webster, waiting to play with the second
foursome on that tee, delivered a steady stream of ribbing and
abuse, as golfers are prone to do. Webster didn't hesitate to
talk in the middle of a swing, a habit that can get a man in
serious trouble in some circles. Apparently, it doesn't matter
in Ozona, even in the big Invitational. Then again, the DPS
team was playing in the second flight. Webster might not have
teased the golfers in the championship flight, and I'll bet he
wouldn't have teased former Southwest Conference champ
Jess Claiborne.

To the right of the first tee, smoke issued from the big
barbecue pit under the mesquite trees and rose almost
straight up in the quiet, early morning air. Bill Glasscock's
briskets simmered on the grill as grease dripped from a hole
into a bucket. Glasscock was surprised when I informed him
that mesquite-grilled barbecue is a prized viand in New York
City and Southampton, and very expensive.

Back on the first tee, Dick Webster's foursome was preparing to tee off as the DPS group cleared the fairway in front
of them. Playing with Webester and his son Rick were J. L.
Alexander, who did most of the paperwork for the tournament, and Randy Poage. Not a rancher in the bunch—Dick
Webster is a businessman, Rick a pumper for an oil and gas
company (a safe job with a good company), Alexander a retired
banker, and Poage an engineer with the highway department
who had lived in Ozona when the interstate was coming
through. Now the highway is finished and Poage lives in Fort
Stockton, where he handles miles and miles of odds and ends.

Rick Webster played golf on the high school team with

David and Mike Williams, and they went a long way in the Double A Tournament in 1971 (the smallest rural schools are A; the urban colossi, Five A). After graduating from high school, Webster played on the Angelo State golf team, and he's still about as good as he ever was: a 2 handicap. I watched closely as he stepped to the tee. Frankly, I wanted to see an interesting golf swing, something offbeat.

Webster gripped the club with a very strong right hand turned way under the shaft, like a touring pro named Ed Fiori who played for the University of Houston. A grip like this might plague a golfer with hooks—too much hand action coming through the ball. Then Webster opened his stance to the target, like Lee Trevino. Then he brought the club back very flat, like Ray Floyd. Then he came under the ball as strongly as you can, again like Floyd. Then he smacked his drive with the authority of all three of those pros. I didn't have to see the landing area in the first fairway to know that this ball was straight down the middle, far away. Closest resemblance to Webster's swing among the pros? Ray Floyd.

Rick's father's swing didn't produce such marvelous results. The ball arced out to the right. Poage hit a long, straight drive with a short swing. Alexander, a tall man, had one of those trusty senior-citizen swings that can make a golfer a lot of money in bets, even though he was loose in the backswing, fairly flipping the club up with his wrists—a nice illustration of Johnny Miller's point that it doesn't matter how you get the club to the top so long as it comes down correctly. (Lanny Wadkins, the fastest-swinging pro, says it doesn't matter how fast you go back so long as you come down *faster.*) After a couple of holes I knew that Alexander almost always hits the ball straight, and not much shorter than the belters on the team, the younger Webster and Randy Poage.

Two routine pars on the first hole for that group. The second hole is a short dogleg right, out-of-bounds right, of course. The tee is set back on a ledge among trees, so the green is out of sight. A nice little hole, although ideally a golf course doesn't start out with two holes requiring blind or semiblind drives. (The opener at Shinnecock Hills is perfect: elevated tee with the green in the distance, the view providing a sense of all there is to see on the course, an invitation to a round of golf.)

Lined up around the third tee I counted twelve golf carts, the first traffic jam of the day. Three foursomes, twelve carts. There were wives and girlfriends riding on some of them. One of the women was Eddie Hall, Randy Hall's wife, a newcomer to these parts. I noticed two golf bags on the cart, and she said that she'd taken up the game after moving from East Texas several years ago, when Hall was transferred. "I knew I had to play golf to live here," she said. "There's nothing else to do."

That was the refrain I heard in Ozona. The reason why so many kids and women as well as men play golf is that there's nothing else to do. Indeed, there's no shopping mall, no movie theater, no bowling alley (though there were a theater and a bowling alley when I was a kid). There are softball diamonds and some tennis courts that get play, and satellite dishes, of course, but golf is the perfect game for that fair-weather part of the country. Everywhere else, the complaint is that golf takes up too much time. "Exactly!" explain the golfers of West Texas.

On that third tee I had the opportunity to watch twelve tee shots on this 190-yard hole. I saw what I'd have seen on any other golf course—all kinds of swings and shots that produced two balls on the green. Fifteen percent of the shots on the green: That's just about the national average for a long par three, I imagine.

J. L. Alexander holed out from off the green for a birdie—the first of the day for his team. Rick Webster picked up the pace and holed birdies on the fourth hole, a long par five straight down the fence line, and the short fifth, which he almost drove. The Webster team finished the front nine four under par, a score deemed respectable but not outstanding.

Horses Williams was playing golf, too, on Saturday morning, teamed with B. W. Stuart, his son Greg Stuart, and their friend Gene Lilly, who is in the oil-field construction business. After a few holes watching this third-flight foursome, I noticed a certain discrepancy in play. Greg Stuart, a big guy, was pounding the ball with a swing like Craig Stadler's. Obviously Stuart didn't belong in the third flight, so I asked what was going on. He explained that he basically wasn't playing much golf anymore, that he'd spent all summer playing softball, and that he was just playing along for the fun of it. I could only conclude that if he did play steadily, he'd be a scratch golfer—a par shooter. Like Rick Williams, the younger Stuart is a pumper in the oil patch.

His father used to be the Chrysler dealer in town, and before that he worked for the Chevy dealership, and I could see this was coming: B. W. Stuart had sold Bailey Post two of the old cars we scooted around town in, one of them a converted taxicab. Now Stuart was a county commissioner—but not for long. The citizens had voted him out, he told me, mainly for spending money on the softball diamonds that were so popular. This confused him because those were federal revenue-sharing funds, not local tax dollars. But, he concluded, "Some people are against everything."

This group, with the exception of Greg Stuart, looked and played about like I remember my father's Texaco foursome: bogey golf. Horses Williams doesn't get through the ball too well anymore, but he doesn't have to in order to play bogey golf. One: down the fairway. Two: down the fairway, closing in. Three: on or almost on the green. Four: chip or putt close.

Five: 2 footer for par. This bogey or better game of the senior golfer relies on straight shots and a dependable short game. I understood that there were some senior golfers in the tournament who were a lot better than that. I'd find them.

Another member of that really good 1971 Double A golf team in Ozona was Jim Montgomery, now a dentist living in San Angelo. Montgomery was playing in the third flight Saturday on a team with Larry Walker, the club's only full-time maintenance man. Many guys who have hung around golf courses in some such capacity have developed good golf games. Walker isn't one of them. His powerful swing can send the ball any which way, and he's good-natured about the results. You have to be cheerful to play golf badly and not quit. (But being cheerful is no guarantee in this regard. I'm relatively cheerful and I've quit golf, or lapsed, several times.)

Jim Montgomery's uncle is Beecher Montgomery, one of Ozona's landed gentry. Beecher was competing in the second flight with a man I was told to be sure to meet, Eddie Hale. Horses Williams said of Eddie Hale, "He's a goat roper."

Hale must be every Yankee's idea of a West Texas golfer (or maybe every Yankee's idea of a West Texas golfer is Bic Benedict—Rock Hudson). He's built like a jockey but a little bigger, a grizzled fellow with a quick grin. He's wiry, from all the goat roping. Hale owns some ranch land, leases more, and competes in rodeos. He was one of the few players playing golf on Saturday wearing blue jeans. Shorts were more popular. (On the patio on Friday night, I was wearing jeans and Mike Williams suggested I was a bit overdressed for the next day's entertainment.)

"Lots of ranchers play golf," Hale explained to me between his many shots. "We're competitive. After we're too worn out for roping and riding, we play golf." Goat roping is just like calf roping, only harder. The little critters are quick—

although not as quick as jackrabbits, which are roped on
unofficial occasions. Earlier in the summer Hale was officiat-
ing at a goat-roping event in San Angelo and had to flag his
own son—disqualify the kid—on the grand prize throw worth
five thousand dollars. Before the time limit had elapsed, the
animal got loose from the knot Eddie Junior had whipped
around his ankles and skittered off.

Hale moves with ease between the rodeo set and the
Ozona Country Club set because they're the same set. Move
into or near Ozona and don't bring with you a reputation for
high crimes and misdemeanors and you're in the country club
if you wish to be. There's certainly old and proud money in
Ozona, as there is at Shinnecock Hills, but in Ozona that
money plays golf with state troopers and car salesmen. However, that money does not play golf with any of the Mexicans
living in town, because none of them are members of the club,
and a couple have tried to join.

"There is, indeed, no way for a stranger to tell the
difference between a millionaire rancher and the man who
pumps gas at the filling station. Each wears a dusty, pearl-gray
sombrero and high-heeled, sharp-pointed boots decorated
with steer heads or floral patterns. Between the boots and the
hat, each adorns himself with a nondescript khaki shirt and
pants known locally as 'duckins,' and each is equally sun-and-
wind-burned to the leathery color and texture of a well-worn
saddle." Six months after that issue of *The Saturday Evening
Post* was published, the author could have seen the same
apparel at the grand opening of the new country club. Thirty-
five years later, it's still about the same. As I rode around the
links in my golf cart, I saw few of the visionary colors the pros
and swank amateurs feel compelled to wear.

Sand greens still exist in Rocksprings, about halfway between Ozona and San Antonio in Edwards County. I found out about them from Epp Epperson, a rancher from Rocksprings who was playing in the third flight. Epperson was wearing a Casa Salsa cap his mother had brought back from a vacation in Cancun. Otherwise he looked like a ranching golfer ought to look (not unlike Rock Hudson, in fact) and his fast, splayed-out swing sometimes produced good shots. He explained how the sand greens work. After a string tied to the flagstick is used to measure the length of the putt, the ball is moved to the one specially dragged area of sand and placed at the appropriate distance from the hole. Thus everyone has the same putt, except for length.

"Sure the greens are small," Epperson said, "but when you hit one, it sticks. And you won't putt the ball past the hole. No putter in the world is made that heavy!" The heavier the putter, the farther the ball rolls with the same rap. Older golfers, including pros, switch to a heavier putter as their touch begins to slip. Heavy putters are a fad in general because they encourage a smooth, easy stroke instead of a jab.

An Epperson putt on the front nine whizzed past the hole. Somebody chided, "That wouldn't have gone in with a weight on it."

"Yeah, but it took the break out of it," Epperson replied.

Maybe Pon Seahorn was the teaser. Pon is short for Ponder, who is one of the bosses at the local bank, the *old* local bank, he hurried to inform me. The new bank, I knew, was a victim of unfortunate timing. It opened just about when the oil prices cratered. And of course it figured that Seahorn is my grandmother's banker—an account without a lot of activity, I imagine.

Playing with Seahorn and Epperson in their third flight group was Seahorn's daughter's date for the day. The kid, a freshman in college, hit the best ball of the group but had a lot to make up for. I would have felt very comfortable with that particular foursome: good shot, bad shot, good, bad. (That's about like Army golf, which is left, right, left, right.)

By the time the morning rounds were completed, I'd seen all of the Ozona golf course, and I liked it a lot. Utterly unaffected, unlike so many (mostly new) courses with their gigantic greens, huge bunkers, artificially rolling fairways, fake blue lakes, everything on an elephantine scale. Ozona is more enjoyable than all of them. I don't say "better" because that's not the issue. Some of them might be better as rated on a scale of strategic values, but a golf course should not look like a theme park. And it has to be fun to play. If Shinnecock Hills and Augusta National aren't fun to play, they're not good golf courses. I believe Bobby Jones would have agreed with the assertion. I'll bet Augusta and Shinnecock are fun to play—but no more fun than Ozona.

Just in time, Mark Harvey arrived from Houston, put on his cleats, and joined David and Mike Williams and Duane Childress for their afternoon round. When I caught up with them, they were all hitting good-to-excellent shots. This was a first-flight foursome on the verge of being championship-flight caliber. They would beat some championship-flight teams on gross score, in fact.

Duane Childress hits the ball like the pro Gary Koch, with a jerk of the hips right at impact. A "power shudder," Childress dubbed it after I pointed out the similarity. The shudder does interrupt the smooth flow of the swing, but Childress drove the ball long and straight most of the round. Mike Williams had the smoothest swing in the group. David whispered to me as we watched his brother set up for a shot, "I'd like to have that swing to work with."

Mark Harvey had the most problems in the group, as stands to reason: He seldom plays anymore. The team ended up the round four under par, tied at the halfway mark with the Dick and Rick Webster team, two behind the leaders.

A scoreboard was posted on the bulletin board on the patio, and the afternoon golfers gathered around after play to drink beer and size up their status. The flighting results on Saturday looked reasonable enough to me. The best score in the first, second, and third flights would have been right about in the middle of the pack in the immediately preceding better flight. Likewise, the worst score in the championship and first flights would have been roughly in the middle of the pack in the next lower flight.

In the championship flight, four teams were within four shots of the lead. I hadn't seen many of the championship players; I would catch them on Sunday. First, though, would come the barbecue and "team discussion" Saturday night.

7

Anyone who remembers his first swipe at a golf ball, or has watched others attempt it, knows immediately that the golf swing is an unnatural and therefore awkward maneuver for the human body. The pros make the swing look like a natural reflex. The best lesson I ever had on this point was delivered one afternoon in an office on Madison Avenue. Johnny Miller was explaining some swing point and jumped out of his chair to demonstrate with a pantomime swing. Even without a club in his hand, his body movement was utterly convincing. The muscles had the swing memorized and they engaged automatically. I thought I heard the *thwack!*

I had learned the same lesson about athletes years earlier, without realizing it. I was writing a story about Roy Harris, the white hope from Cut 'n' Shoot, Texas, who fought Floyd Patterson for the heavyweight championship in 1958. He knocked the champion down in the fourth round but lost on a TKO in the twelfth. The former contender is now a lawyer and the county clerk of Montgomery County, north of Houston, where I worked for the daily newspaper. Harris was sitting behind his desk when he decided to demonstrate some point of technique with the left hook. He got up and walked around, stood me up, took his position, feinted with the right, and then reached out and tapped me on the shoulder with the left. A tap, nothing more, but it almost knocked me down.

The muscles had engaged automatically; he was swinging from his heels.

The golf pro's swing is the product of a lifetime of hours spent on the practice tee. Even the pros who "don't practice much" practice a lot—a whole lot, earlier in their careers. The practice tee is where any golfer gets better, and that's the main reason most amateur players never get better. They don't practice, or don't practice well, because it's work, not fun.

My father is the classic case. He'll spend half an hour on the putting green, and he's a good putter, but he won't hit balls on the practice tee; he just doesn't like to. Several million golfers subscribe to the major golfing publications, and all of them demand instruction, a new story every month about curing the slice. The only reason the magazines publish other stuff, too, is for the sanity of the editors. The readers wouldn't miss any of it. But after all these years of instruction, all the millions of lessons from pros, all the secrets discovered and tips shared, the average handicap of the readers remains the same: 18. Bogey golf. (The official average handicap for all golfers, as determined by the National Golf Foundation, is slightly higher: 22.1 for men, 33.8 for women.)

Without diligent practice, all that instruction is smoke and mirrors. The pros seem to be the only golfers who understand this. The practice tee at a pro tournament is not the place to see real golf any more than the batting cage is the place to see baseball, but the practice tee is the place to see and study the polished, finely tuned and reliable power golf swing. In a way it's more reliable than racing engines: At the Indy 500 a couple of weeks before the Open at Shinnecock Hills, only fifteen of thirty-three cars were still running at the end.

The pro hits many dozen, sometimes hundreds of balls in a practice session. He usually starts with soft shots struck with the lofted clubs, shots requiring maximum control instead of distance. (All shots require control; some also require distance.) After he's loose and prepared to generate more power, the pro switches to the longer clubs. Mac O'Grady is an exception. He'll start with the driver. However, he was swinging in front of the mirror before he came to the club. Lon Hinkle is another exception. A big, genial player who hasn't fulfilled expectations on the tour, who lists reading and piano as special interests, Hinkle heads straight for the longer clubs, too, and I don't believe he swings in the hotel room.

The pro works his way up to the woods, the shots the fans enjoy watching the most. The swing repeats and the ball rockets off the clubface with a satisfying *thwack!*—except in the case of the players who hit the metal woods that produce the funny *ping.* And the metal woods are increasingly the clubs of choice for the pros, because most of them hit those clubs a little farther and perhaps a little straighter. The power swing of the pros has produced a power game on the tour. Distance is important. They have to keep up with the Joneses, of whom there are more and more on the tour every year: long hitters.

All average handicap golfers should play with metal woods, for distance and accuracy, and eventually we will. However, many of us simply don't like that silly sound and will wait till the wood we have rots.

Forget the *ping* and consider the *thwack!* The regular player will never produce this sound, even playing good golf. He doesn't hit the ball with enough authority—a combination of strength, tempo, and timing. In addition, the pros hit a high-compression ball, and the backs of their clubs are loaded down with lead tape, as Andy North explained to me years ago. My sound with his club would have been a *clink.*

An amateur would be thrilled with almost every shot the pros strike, on the practice tee or the golf course, but the pros say they hit as many bad shots as anyone. Theirs just aren't as bad. Ben Hogan claimed he was satisfied with, at most, only half a dozen shots in a round. My friend Gene Keogh, one of the Brooklyn foursome who now plays at one of those private clubs in Westchester County, overheard Curtis Strange remark to a friend after an under-par round at the Bob Hope event in California, "It's a sin to play so bad." Indeed, the pros will often shoot a four-under 68, report that they didn't play well at all, and then retire to the practice tee to work on that hitch in the swing. The workday ends where it began.

The absolute worst shot you'll see a pro hit in a practice session is some kind of bad fade that's not quite a slice, or a bad hook that's not quite a jerk. But as often as not after what appears to be a fine shot, the pro expresses displeasure as he peers down the line of flight. He scowls, steps back, inquires of his attending caddie what went wrong to cause the ball to land twenty feet left of a target 175 yards away. The caddie is the mirror as his boss maneuvers his body, shifts his hips, fiddles with the all-important grip of the hands on the shaft, investigates the shoulder turn, also all-important, worries about his feet, his knees, his head, everything. It's all all-important. There is no rest. The body is different every day. So is the swing.

So are the clubs. If the pro can't find the flaw in his swing, he can seek it in his clubs. Winston Churchill grumbled after a hapless round that the golf club is ill-suited to the purpose. The pros are able to meet this problem head-on. At every tournament, craftsmen working for various manufacturers set up shop in mobile vans. Experts in club analysis, repair, and modification, equipped with measuring devices and tools, they can make the tiniest alterations in the angles and weights of golf clubs. Dollar (now Senator) Bill Bradley, the former New York Knickerbocker, was renowned for his ability to discern that the basket was half an inch high or low, based on the results of a set of shots. The golf pro knows when the loft on his iron has been stressed out of alignment by a degree or two, and he'll get it fixed.

Before I settled down on the bleachers behind the practice tee at Shinnecock Hills on Monday, I stepped onto the golf course and encountered Herman Mitchell, Lee Trevino's famous caddie, walking off the seventh green. He was out checking the greens and the pin placements for the practice round. That is diligence. For tournament rounds the caddies are provided with a schematic chart showing each of the eighteen greens and the yardage of that day's pin placements from the front, back, and each side of the green. Reliable caddies go one step further and proceed onto the course with chart in hand to augment the footage with information on the topography of the green relative to the specific pin location. Example: The hole on the second green might be on a slight knob, with the green falling away from that area to the back and right. The caddie will remind his player of this, and the pro will try to keep his ball on the flatter portion of the green, to the left and in front of the flag. Basic strategy during a tournament, but I was still surprised to see Mitchell out on the course on the first practice day of the week.

One of the few fans around called out to him, "Where's the boss?" Like most fans, he knew this big man with an enormous girth was Lee Trevino's caddie.

"How do I know where the boss is?" Mitchell retorted without grace, then padded off toward another green, mumbling, "Where's the boss!? Where's the boss!?"

It stood to reason that the boss was back on the practice tee, dressed all in brown, hitting golf balls with his too-flat swing, his legs too far apart and too open to the target. No one has ever hit golf balls better with a worse-looking contraption. It's easy to see how Trevino cleaned up in hustling matches before he joined the tour, including a match in El Paso with Raymond Floyd.

As I watched Trevino hit balls, Alistair Cooke arrived on the scene. Golf writer and host of "Masterpiece Theatre," he was properly attired in jacket and tie and white sneakers. I once edited a piece Cooke wrote about the traditions of The Masters. I use the verb "edited" quite loosely. I was afraid to change one word, and didn't, in part because I had been recently abused over the telephone by another famous sportswriter who had profiled a top pro for the magazine. I thought I'd merely "tightened" the piece; he complained that I made his fine prose read like *Newsweek*. I expected to see only one person other than Cooke wearing a jacket and tie at the Open—not counting Shinnecock Hills members, who might have felt so obliged. That would be Herbert Warren Wind, venerable golf writer for *The New Yorker*, the grand old man in the field; our answer, in a later generation, to Bernard Darwin. But all in all, there's no question that Britain has produced superior golf writing, stylish stuff. In America, the best sportswriters have taken up baseball; that's the official explanation.

Not surprisingly, a British writer came up with the most canny description of Lee Trevino's golf swing: *agricultural*. That's the right word to conjure images of Trevino's apparently undisciplined thrashing. Hackers have better-looking swings than his. *I* had a lot better-looking swing. Better looking, that is, until you really look closely. A lot of strange things can happen on the backswing and the follow through of a golf swing so long as everything comes together correctly in the impact zone. Golf swings look so different because we're seeing mostly backswing and follow through. But at the moment of impact, every good swing is quite similar: the head still, the body and legs driving *through* (not around), the shoulder driving *under* (not around), the arms and the club-head propelled by the centrifugal force generated by the legs and the body. The stop-action comparisons used by the network broadcasts show all this clearly.

Lee Trevino certainly utilizes strong action from his big hips and thighs, but he also unquestionably employs his hands in the impact zone. This makes him, in the jargon, a "hitter." Nicklaus is a "swinger": He hits the ball with his legs and his body and his arms. He has no real concept of hitting it with his hands. Most golf swings can be identified as either hitter or swinger. The key is the hands at impact: Hitters *hit* the ball—it's obvious—while swingers forget the ball, which just happens to get in the way of their smooth pass. However, Nicklaus did say that he was so perfectly tuned at the U. S. Open at Pebble Beach in 1972 that he could make fine adjustments with his hands as he was moving into the ball. Trevino uses that gift most of the time.

"Superbly coordinated hands have been responsible for some great golf," Nicklaus wrote in one of his instruction books, "but unskilled hands dominating the swing is a prime cause for high handicaps." When I read that, I knew I'd been going about the golf swing all wrong, no matter how sweet, pure, and untutored mine might have looked. I wasn't really hitting the ball with that swing. I was hitting it with my hands, and unintentionally at that. I was flinching, I think: a loss-of-confidence flinch right at impact. When I played well for a stretch, it was only because I had momentarily hot hands, with the rest of me cool under fire. With exquisite feel and a great deal of practice Trevino can get away with that action, to say the least. I was silly to expect to. But for me and all the other millions of average handicap golfers, the urge to do *something* with the hands, the most immediate source of contact with the ball via the club, is irresistible. We can't forget the ball. The practice required to develop a trustworthy "swing" is beyond our dedication. (Soccer players might make great "swinging" golfers because they're used to athletic activity that doesn't directly involve their hands. They think with their legs, like Nicklaus.)

British Open champion Sandy Lyle walked over to Trevino's position on the practice tee, and they engaged in an evaluation of hip movement, or so I judged from the body gestures. The pros never quit thinking about the basics. Just as dancers work at the bar every day on the *pro forma* material, golfers exchange ideas on fundamentals they have perfected—relative to amateurs—years before. The pros are competitors, but the atmosphere at tournaments is collegial, and players often attribute victory to some tip received the previous week from another player.

Lyle is a big, strong guy with a funny little loop at the top of his shorter-than-usual backswing, but everything is in order when he returns the club to the ball. He's one of the longest hitters in the game. In contrast to Trevino's agricultural swing, Lyle's swing is *industrial*. Andy Bean, Craig Stadler, and Greg Norman also have industrial swings. These are big guys who pound the ball with a simple, workmanlike stroke: put the clubhead on the ball and with all that mass or muscle or both behind the effort, the ball has to move out. Pro shops post the famous—and sexist—cartoon of the teaching pro giving a lesson to a hefty woman. The pro sets his pupil at address and says whimsically, "Now just shift that weight."

The good industrial golf swing seems to undercut the old adage about tempo and timing being more important than strength as a source of power. However, there are big men who don't hit the ball a long way. True industrialists have tempo and timing, too.

A third basic kind of pro swing is the new-fangled product of the country clubs and colleges. I call this the *corporate* golf swing. (Thus all golf is divided into three parts: agricultural, industrial, and corporate.) It is all smoothness and pace and very proper technique, groomed from an early age with the help of professional teachers. The ultimate corporate swing belonged to Jerry Pate (past tense because a shoulder injury ruined it). Pate won the U. S. Open his first year on the tour, in 1976. Effortless was the only description for his pass at the ball, with absolutely no action of the hands apparent at the bottom of the swing. It was a marvelous golf swing.

While hitting and swinging are distinctions between golf swings only, the agricultural-industrial-corporate nomenclature describes not only the swing but also a way of playing the game, and the golfer's personality as well. Trevino's agricultural swing was cooked up on public layouts in Texas. Eccentricity is often the hallmark of such swings—learned without much, if any, professional teaching, perfected on public courses that usually aren't in good shape, where bad lies necessitate imagination. These swings are almost always quicker and uglier than the more refined products of the country clubs and colleges. (But Calvin Peete's is not; his publinks swing is slow and stately, if idiosyncratic in other respects.)

Most of the touring pros today have some kind of industrial swing, a middle ground between the rude success of the agriculturalists and the Xeroxed efficiency of the corporate players. The proponents of the industrial swing also tend to be the middle generation, between the agricultural swing of an older generation and the corporate swing that's the rage on the campuses—and thus increasingly on the tour.

The corporate swings are near-clones of one another. Some writers and fans complain that the younger pros are clones in other respects, too: articulate without being interesting, overly conscious of their media image, not very creative on the course. Certainly the younger players aren't shotmakers in the manner of Trevino and Floyd, golfers who can create an answer right on the course. The one great exception is Severiano Ballesteros, twenty-eight years old, who grew up with the game in the old way, hacking away with whatever clubs he could find in Santander, Spain. Nevertheless, his beautiful swing belongs with the *Fortune* 500. He has the fullest, smoothest shoulder turn of any player; his spine is constructed of ball bearings. You feel the hands working at impact, but gently. The same softness with which he handles the club on the short shots is somehow apparent on the full strikes, too. He holds the driver as tenderly as he holds his putter, and he swings the big club with just about the same fluid pace.

Sam Snead? Yes, his incomparable swing is still smooth in a corporate way at seventy-four years of age, but I won't put that label on him. His swing was bred in the bone, and that's different.

Seve Ballesteros is the premier magician in the game today. Mechanics/magicians. That's another popular and fairly valid means of distinguishing between excellent golfers. (Duffers are just duffers.)

Mechanics concentrate on perfecting the technicalities of the swing. They work hard to engrave muscle memory, warrantied by thousands of hours on the practice tee. Ben Hogan, master mechanic, could approach a line of one dozen golf balls and address each one in turn—swing, step forward, swing, step forward—and his caddie, stationed 175 yards away, would snare almost every ball in his big white towel and barely miss the other few. That's muscle manipulation and memory of an astonishing order, considering that a change of just three degrees in the angle of the clubface striking the ball results in an aberration of 10 yards when the ball lands 175 yards away. That's a pretty tiny error for the human body to control, but a devastating result for the golfer who would be a pro. Add to this depressing information a consideration of the other vectors operating at impact: the angle of incline of the clubhead's path, the angle of the clubface tilting in the vertical plane, and clubhead speed. The timing is not split-second. It's split-millisecond. Finally, consider the body mechanics responsible for these vectors: arms, legs, torso, neck and head, wrists and hands working to produce explosive power—the clubhead accelerated to well over a hundred miles per hour—while maintaining dozens of precise alignments.

When I think about it, it's a miracle that my every shot isn't slugged into the water. And if I *do* think about it during the swing, the ball will certainly splash. The body and the brain cannot consciously control everything that's happening as the body releases the power. Common sense supports the "swinging" over the "hitting" method, hard as it is to pull off: Set the body in good address position, follow a couple of basic swing keys on the takeaway to a predictable position at the top, engage a couple of other keys on the downswing, and then just let it happen. The awesomely technical Golfing Machine strategy formerly advocated by pros Mac O'Grady and Bobby Clampett called for very conscious control during the downswing, keyed by the sensations received in the index finger of the right hand. O'Grady dropped that course of study when he became convinced that such perception and control are physically impossible in the time allotted.

Hogan was a swinger, but he developed a reliable stroke

only after years of struggle, rebuilding a swing that early in his career produced too many crooked shots (hooks, of course). Hogan didn't win an event until his eighth year on the tour, and he didn't hit full stride for six or seven years more—until he was almost forty. Young pros can take solace from that history if they have the fortitude and the cash reserves, but Hogan's era isn't today's. There weren't nearly as many good golfers then. Such late blooming might not happen again, although it just did, if not quite so dramatically, for Calvin Peete.

The magicians like Ballesteros are more laid back, and perhaps more gifted. They place more faith in their intuitively felt symbiosis of body and brain. However, this mental-side legerdemain requires a decent swing to trust in: See the visual image of the flight of the ball, feel the swing necessary to produce that shot, trust the body to deliver the goods. Not for Seve Ballesteros—who was hitting astounding shots as a young teenager—the tedious, cold-blooded construction of a robot's swing. He doesn't hit the ball straight down the middle, and maybe he doesn't want to all the time. But he has the sorcerer's resources to hit a shot from a parking lot—which he did to win the British Open at Royal Lytham in 1979. (Accused of being outrageously wild on his drive on that hole, he had actually aimed for the parking lot, a shortcut where he knew the grass was matted down.)

Alas, Seve's bag of tricks can play tricks on him. He probably lost The Masters in 1986 to Nicklaus when he chunked his 4-iron approach shot into the water on the fifteenth hole: a pull hook, unbelievably bad for a pro, something I'd be more likely to produce. And it followed a marvelous shot with a 6-iron, to a more difficult target on the thirteenth hole, which he eagled.

Ballesteros was dressed in purple when he strode onto the practice tee Monday morning, carrying his own bag. The fans sitting in the bleachers watched in quiet reverence as he passed by. And soon Herman Mitchell joined Lee Trevino after completing his tour of the golf course. When he walked the length of the tee to fetch another bag of balls, a man called out, "Is Lee gonna hit another bag?"

"I'm not doing this for the exercise," Mitchell snorted.

"You need it," the fan laughed.

Say that on a street corner and you might get flattened. Mitchell glared at the man but didn't say a word.

Also present on the range:

- Sam Randolph, the defending Amateur Champion, itching to turn pro. (Four of the five amateurs in the field were would-be pros, and the fifth, Bob Lewis, is a former pro.) Randolph's swing is rather clunky, a rarity among the new batch of assembly-line models. He takes the club back very slowly, then strikes the ball with a quick, surprising lurch.

- Fred Funk, a vision in pale green who doesn't have a namesake swing after all. Basic corporate golf. Coach at Maryland.

- The Chen brothers from Taiwan: Tze-Chung, who almost won our Open in 1985, and Tze-Ming, who defeated Tom Watson in a playoff in 1983 to win a big tournament in Japan. These brothers from another continent have practically identical 5-foot-10, 145-pound, flat-chested golf swings. (Likewise, Curtis Strange and his twin brother Allan, golfer of nearly-pro caliber, have just about the same swing. However, Tom Kite, Ben Crenshaw, and Tom Watson are within an inch of each other in height and five pounds in weight, with a similar physique, but their swings are very different. Blood tells.)

- Jack Renner, the skinny pro who lifts his shoulders ever so slightly just before he initiates the backswing, even on little chips. Andy Bean lifts a fraction, too. This can't be ideal. All the body's weight in a golf swing should be moving downward, even as the arms are moving upward in the backswing. But a golf swing with a solid or even not-so-solid foundation may be a series of perfected compensations. Most of them are.

Practicing on Tuesday:

● Michael Colandro, a pro I'd never seen, with the spiffiest outfit of the day. From the top down: white hat, black shirt, white sweater, black plus fours, white hose, black and white shoes, while working out of a green and white golf bag. He couldn't wear these clothes anywhere else. Why do golfers wear them on the golf course? The flashy clothes really started with debonair Jimmy Demaret after World War II, when, perhaps, the society wanted to loosen up, and the style caught on.

● Payne Stewart, working down the row from Colandro. Stewart is the most notoriously flashy dresser among the pros; his trademark is the plus fours (Colandro isn't well enough known for his to be a trademark). But Stewart dresses up only on tournament days. On Tuesday he was "incognito," as Ben Crenshaw once joked. Stewart's record demonstrates how difficult it is to win on the tour. Twenty-nine years old, solid swing, very long hitter, good putter, he had only two victories in six years on the tour. If he has a major problem, it might be the short putts. He missed a couple of tiny ones in the British Open in 1985 and finished second to Sandy Lyle by a single stroke. His next win could be at Shinnecock Hills, since he almost always plays well in the majors.

● Tom Kite practicing with his dippy swing. I don't know what it is about Kite's pass at the ball: He hits it far enough, but the swing looks—well—dippy, with a little lift at the top.

● Scott Verplank, thought to be "the next Nicklaus" until *Sports Illustrated* did a cover story on number-three son,

Gary Nicklaus, and gave him that title. Just turned pro, Verplank had not yet covered his bag with a bunch of sponsors' decals. Verplank is a hitter, not a swinger, with powerful hand and body action through the ball. It's not a corporate or an agricultural swing. Rather, it's a corporate-type swing without the smoothly functioning bureaucracy—closer to industrial except that Verplank is not big enough to power the truly industrial swing. In short, the swing doesn't look all that smooth and coordinated to me, but of course that means nothing. As the only amateur to win a tour event in many years (the 1985 Western Open in Chicago), Verplank can play. VERPLANK KERPLUNK read the headlines. He was hitting his drives all over the place downrange on Tuesday, and he might have been aiming in all those different directions, but he didn't look happy. He was hitting Ping clubs. Pings were dismissed by the pros for many years as "game improvement" clubs, designed to help the bad swings that don't consistently strike the ball with the sweet spot of the clubhead. With game-improvement clubs, more of the mass of the clubhead is moved to the perimeter, so the sweet spot is more diffused. This, the pros reasoned, couldn't be good for them. But Verplank plays Pings. Bob Tway plays Pings. And Jack Montgomery told me in Houston that fully eighty percent of all college players are now playing Pings.

● Dan Pohl, whacking long drives with his ultrashort backswing and very little wrist cock at the top. Pohl cocks the wrists on his downswing, using a strongly pronated left wrist. He releases with the pent-up torque of a crossbow.

● Sandy Lyle, with a swing about as short as Pohl's but using a completely different release mechanism, or so it appears. Lyle seems to generate his power simply with his size. On Monday he'd been in deep discussion with Trevino on hip action. On Tuesday he was hitting a series of 1-irons off the tee. Perhaps he planned to drive with that club on certain holes, and perhaps he wanted to fade that shot left-to-right. He might hit that faded l-iron with a bucket of balls or more, trying to set it in the mind and the muscles. A spectator sitting behind me in the stands watched Lyle hit and announced, "That's too conservative for this course. He'll never make it." The man was talking through his hat. Apparently he believed that Lyle was planning on driving with the 1-iron, which he deemed a mistake. But he had no idea how the golf course set up for the pros, and he didn't know that Lyle hits the 1-iron as far as many pros hit their drivers (Johnny Miller, who had switched to a metal driver for the Open, made that specific observation to me). And the fan didn't know whether Lyle even intended to hit the club in the tournament; he might have been working on some swing factor that makes itself particularly evident with a long-iron. Who knows? Certainly not the fan.

● Portly Bob Murphy (from Brooklyn), working on his swing, which features the slowest takeaway of all, followed by an agonizing pause at the top that would be the death of most players. When we get up there, we've got to get going immediately; the suspense is killing us. But Murphy is in no hurry. He has a wonderful putting touch, too, with a very slow stroke. Players with slow swings, like Murphy and Frank Conner, bring to mind the inimitable Julius Boros, now a quite senior golfer who had what appeared to be the most effortless golf swing ever—as effortless as Jerry Pate's and a lot slower. My unaided eye couldn't see how Boros's swing generated much power, but it did. Massive arms and hands and good action with his body were the secret. That swing never changed; neither did Boros's expression as he moved placidly about the course like a cold-blooded creature. While other golfers would fuss over potential distractions, Boros simply got up to his ball and hit it. On putts he didn't always care to clear the leaves from his line. I liked Boros but had a hard time forgiving him for beating Palmer in a playoff for the Open in 1963.

● Miller Barber. His good friend and fellow Texan Crenshaw once said that Barber looks as if he has hooked the club on a clothesline at the top of the backswing. His hands loop and the elbows fly in all directions—but then everything moves into the ball with, as Sam Snead pointed out, "perfect balance." (Johnny Miller threatens to play a round of tournament golf without using any backswing. He would just lift the club into position at the top and swing down from there. He argues that the purpose of the traditional backswing is to get the club up in the correct position at the top. If you can get it there otherwise, fine.) There's no secret why Miller Barber now plays better than his more famous contemporary Arnold Palmer. Palmer's swing was always fast and furious and dependent on superb timing—and a magical putting stroke to save the day. It never stood a prayer of holding up under tournament pressure for thirty years. Barber's swing, while weird looking at the top, has that perfect balance, and is actually quite simple, easy to control, and long lasting. He qualified for the 1986 Open as defending Senior Open Champion. Palmer tried but failed to qualify and said it would be his last attempt. (Former champions get a ten-year exemption from subsequent Opens, but no more. After that and other exemptions expired for Palmer, the USGA gave him several "special exemptions," and the first year the USGA didn't grant him one, the fans raised a ruckus. Palmer defended the USGA position. If I'm not playing well enough to qualify, he said, then I shouldn't be in the tournament.)

● Ray Floyd, forty-three years old, staking out a position on the tee. Floyd is one of the most tenacious players in the game. He has an agricultural swing, but one very different from Trevino's. Trevino takes the clubhead outside the target line on his backswing—breaking a rule—and then reroutes it coming down. Floyd takes the club away radically inside the line, very flat and very quickly, and his weight shift looks like some kind of dance. Agricultural, but reaping great rewards: nineteen victories, including the PGA Championship (twice), The Masters, and the Tournament Players Championship.

● Big Jim Thorpe and his muscle-bound swing. Thorpe is the leading contradiction of the essentially sound idea that golfing muscles need to be lithe, free, and unbundled. He crushes the ball with a powerful, low punch and a Palmer-like waggle in his follow through.

● Cal Peete, an essay in beige. Paparazzi crowded around as Peete walked slowly past the pro shop and onto the practice tee. A handsome couple asked him to pause for a picture. He did so and flashed a smile. When a pro addresses a genuine greeting to a fan, everyone around treats it as a benediction. The recipient shines with reflected fame-glow, and his or her neighbors in the gallery look on with new respect. Normally Peete signs autographs with a carefully constructed no-face. It's easy to understand the no-face defensiveness of besieged golfers such as Peete who must plow through hordes of autograph seekers to get to the tee, the locker room, the car. But I wonder about the young pros whom nobody knows but who have already perfected the superstar's detachment. (Many years ago I watched Johnny Carson from backstage. As he approached the set from his dressing room, his features were set in concrete, completely immobile. When the red light flashed, he turned on. When the light went off, so did he. This didn't look to me like a great way to live.)

● Seve Ballesteros and Bernhard Langer, hitting shots next to each other. Ballesteros's wedges, Langer's drives: Each ball was in the air for six to seven seconds. I wondered whether this meant anything, perhaps that each club imparted the same energy to the ball, in one case *up*, in the other *out*.

● Dave Eichelberger, with a short backswing and a sweeping motion something like Curtis Strange's. He was working on completely rebuilding his golf swing—in the forty-third year of his life and his nineteenth on the tour. Eichelberger played so poorly in 1985 that he lost his tournament privileges. Someone at Shinnecock Hills asked him what he was doing these days. "Playing golf," he replied. "What else is there to do?" Eichelberger is a testimony to dedication, to put a positive light on it, and he was playing well enough to qualify for the Open. I was rooting for him to win.

8

Rumor was afoot and heading my way. In the bleachers behind the practice tee, word spread that Tom Watson was heading for the first tee. His fans began leaving, but Watson hadn't come to the practice tee yet and I doubted he would tee off before hitting some balls. Pros always warm up unless they're in danger of missing a tee time. Minutes later, Watson and his caddie Bruce Edwards strode onto the practice tee. For all of Tom Watson's hard work and his thirty-six tournament victories, he has never been considered a particularly solid ball striker. Students of the game and Watson's peers acknowledge his wonderful short game. Every fan remembers his incredible chip into the hole on the seventeenth green to beat Nicklaus in the '82 Open at Pebble Beach—the most famous single golf shot of recent memory, but that birdie was meaningful only because Watson had holed or beautifully lagged a series of great putts on the back nine. (I was sitting in a bar in New Jersey after my regular game with the Brooklyn foursome when Watson's wedge went in. We roared with astonishment. I sorely wanted Nicklaus to win, though, just as I used to root for the Yankees when Mickey Mantle played, just as I died when Palmer handed the Open to Billy Casper in 1966.)

In the months before Shinnecock Hills, Watson's game was coming around slowly after a drought of several years; he reiterated this hope a hundred times during the spring. In other words, he was putting better, he thought.

Several years ago I was observing George Archer, one of the best putters in the game, stroking a long, long series of 10 footers. During a break he explained to me the direct correlation, in his experience, between serious time on the practice putting green and success on the golf course. When he was through, he looked over and remarked, "But when a long putt goes in, what is it, really? Magic."

After the quick, explosive bursts of power on the tee and fairway, the game of golf always comes down to those minute expenditures of energy called putts. Almost anyone in the world is physically capable of being the best putter in the world. There's nothing to it, physically. Given a certain level of hand-eye coordination, putting is nothing but a matter of composure. Nerves are what putting is all about. This is most clearly evident with a golfer who has the yips—equal to the shank in its heinousness. A golfer with the yips has difficulty drawing the blade back for a tap in—he might "tap it in" four feet past the hole. His nerves simply cannot program the muscles on a fine enough level. It's painful to watch.

Ben Hogan had the yips late in his career and said that he regretted that the other players had to watch him putt. (I'm sure they didn't.) Asked if he had had any luck correcting the problem, he replied, "Do you know where I could get a new head?" Bernhard Langer, winner of The Masters in 1985, was one of the youngest good players ever to have the yips on the short putts. When he was eighteen (he's now twenty-nine), he hit a downhill 30 footer almost twenty-five feet past the hole. From that moment on, Langer battled the yips. He was written up in science journals: "dysfunction of basal ganglia." Four years after the onset of the symptoms, Seve Ballesteros picked up Langer's putter and said, "It's too light." He commanded Langer to switch to something heavier. The problem was solved.

Nerves, yes, but magic, too, because no amount of soft touch can control all the variables affecting the roll of a ball across a carpet of grass. On a 45 footer the odds of some perturbation affecting the roll must be infinitely great. But certain pros will time and again sink the putt they have to, or forget the one they missed and sink the next one. They're better at shutting out the pressure, or turning it around, or something—for a week or a month or a year, or for many years, in the exceptional cases of the greatest putters. The composure and the magic must be connected in some mysterious way—except at the U. S. Open, where no player has ever sunk a putt longer than five feet on the last hole to win. Bobby Jones sank a 15 footer to tie for the championship in 1929, and proceeded to win the playoff. Nicklaus sank a 15 footer on the seventeenth hole to sew up the 1980 Open at Baltusrol. And Tom Watson sank his incredibly deft chip shot at Pebble Beach, in beating an admittedly devastated Nicklaus. But on the final green? This putt to win? Andy North's short one at Cherry Hills in 1978 was as long as any—and long enough, I'm sure. Meanwhile, the list of players who have missed critical putts on the final green is a who's who of the pro game.

The pros have decided that the ephemeral, magical side of the game is worth some attention. More and more of them, including some corporate players, are eschewing the strictly mechanical approach and investigating the darker regions. The top players of professional golf all have excellent games. They're all the best. So why do a few of them win an inordinate number of tournaments—not like the tennis stars, but more than their fair share, given the leveling nature of the game?

Hitting the shots is only part of golf. Playing the game goes way beyond that. How one plays the game dictates how one will play the shots—not vice versa. The mental side of the game, they call it, the part that hard work on the practice tee doesn't help. Sometimes it is sheer magic: Things happen—and putts fall—that you have no explanation for.

In May of 1984, Peter Jacobsen began working with the "imaging techniques" of a psychologist in his home state of Oregon. See a deep canal leading from the ball to the hole, from which the putted ball could not possibly escape; see the hole one foot across, impossible to miss (the real one is 4¼ inches); see the line of the putt bordered by towering sequoias. Take your choice—create your own positive image— then see it clearly and believe it.

One week after Jacobsen had created his own visual mantras, and when he thought his father was dying of cancer, he played in the Colonial Tournament in Fort Worth, Texas.

"I said to myself, 'Let's just win this one for Dad. Let's just let it happen.'"

Everything fell into place. He floated through the week. Following his mentor's advice, he saw the shot, he played the shot. He saw the next one, he played it. No past, no future. No hope, no fear. No consequences: the effortless confidence and action of the child's mind. He won the tournament and his father didn't die. Jacobsen was hot for almost two months. He tied for sixth at the Open at Winged Foot, then won again at the Sammy Davis, Jr.–Greater Hartford Open in Connecticut. But that was two years before Shinnecock Hills, two winless years. In January, he told me he'd been trying too hard, forgetting an essential tenet of most mental-side strategies: The golfer must let it happen.

On the more mundane side, these are the oft-quoted words of advice from Charlie Thom, the club pro at Shinnecock Hills in the old days, to steel magnate Andrew Mellon: "Now there's the ball. Don't be letting your mind wander over to Europe and thinking of what money's to be made over there. The ball's here, so keep your mind on it till you hit it."

Big books have been written on the mental side, all with the same general theme: There's a limit to what alignments and postures and all the other swing mechanics can accomplish; at some point, the golfer has to move into the mistier realm of the alignments and mechanics of the mind. These books don't say it, but the better the golfer is to begin with, the better his chances in the twilight zone. This, too, is where I fall down. When I swing a golf club, my body has a fulcrum—even though I use my hands too much. It's some other kind of center I'm missing, one I'll have to find before I can do much good on the course.

Sportswriters often turn to purple prose when explaining how Nicklaus goes into something of a trance on the course, signaled by the proverbial "look of eagles" in his blue eyes. I don't think it's anything like a trance. If it were, he wouldn't have had tears in his eyes on those last holes at The Masters in 1986, as the huge crowds cheered their hero with a visceral passion. No, it's not a trance. Rather, it's an ability to harness his energies when the time arrives. Nicklaus still swings, walks, waits, and tightens his shoelaces with an aggressive composure—that's his look of eagles. At the heart of Nicklaus's game is an extraordinary finely tuned sense of self. Meet the man, and you feel it instantly: the energy rushing out in a riptide of will and determination.

I think that's the opposite of a trance, and this capacity is vital in an enterprise like golf, with those devastating periods of dead time between shots when tension builds, doubt gnaws, and anger can incapacitate. Nicklaus hasn't read and doesn't need to read books about the mental side of golf because they have nothing to teach him. Let the others try to learn what he knows. Sam Snead was born with the swing for the game; Nicklaus was born with the head for it.

No one has ever been better than Nicklaus at concentrating on that task with as close to one hundred percent of his energies as is humanly possible—and in the next moment talking about the tarpon he caught off the Great Barrier Reef. The awestruck among us label this genius, and why not? An element of genius is surely focused mental energy. At the least, genius issues *from* that focus and cannot exist without it. Chi Chi Rodriguez said about Nicklaus: "A legend in his spare time."

Tom Watson radiates an entirely different feeling. He has said that he's jumping out of his skin during the big tournaments, and this electricity is palpable on the golf course. The other pros don't find this white-hot intensity nearly as intimidating as Nicklaus's cool radiation, but they lost to Watson with great regularity when his putter was performing. Nerves strung taut, Watson nevertheless strides (or strode) the golf course with supreme confidence. The boxer Roy Harris told me that the reason the loser in a bout so often mumbles from beneath his bandages that he should have won, or really did win, is that the man truly believes it. How else, Harris asked me, could anyone get into the ring with a deadly heavyweight? He must believe he's the better boxer.

Jack Nicklaus was asked before the Open at Shinnecock Hills whether the Grand Slam (winning all four majors) was in the back of his mind. No, he said, it was in the front. The great golfers know they'll lose many more tournaments than they'll win. They know this, but they don't *believe* it.

The endeavors of Nicklaus and Watson would seem to relate to I. V. Babbitt's and my own petty pilgrimage about the way Saint Francis's corresponds to Jerry Falwell's. But there's another possibility. Maybe these gods of the game are just athletes after all, good at what they do with their bodies, mostly, with superb powers of concentration and diligence on the practice tee—qualities not for sale, granted, but not the mother lode either. Maybe that look of eagles is just a squint in the bright sunlight. While golf writers like to rhapsodize about the inner strengths of the pros—and I do it, too, sometimes—I know full well that many par shooters (including Nicklaus) accomplish the feat without providing the least evidence that they're concerned with the mystical center that I find mysteriously lacking in my own encounters with the game.

The pro game, it would seem to be an entirely different game, but I'm not sure. I'm not even sure what the difference is between a *violin* and a 5-iron, much less between Nicklaus's 5-iron and my own. Here we are at the famous Amadeus question: How could the blasphemous Mozart produce the wonderful music of the heavens? The pious, furious, less talented Salieri was never informed. One answer is that it's a matter of *talent*, that's all. Fun-loving, freewheeling Lee Trevino, so great without apparently trying, would be golf's Mozart. Salieri would be—too many to list.

I might get a grip on my problems on the golf course some day and be in for a rude surprise. I might play good golf and find out that . . . nothing is revealed, as Bob Dylan testified a couple of generations back.

Mid-morning on the Monday before the tournament at Shinnecock Hills, I saw Peter Jacobsen on the sixth tee. I've talked with Jacobsen a total of maybe five times, and the last time had been in Los Angeles six months earlier. I'm probably one of a hundred golf writers he knows, and one of the thousands of people he's met over the years.

"Hi, Mike," he said instantly. I thought perhaps his work with the mental side of the game was showing results across the board. No, he said, he's always had a memory that good. Jacobsen is one of the stars of pro golf, more famous than his three victories in ten years might warrant. He's famous because he's a comic, a mimic, a personality, and an entertainer of the first order (and name-knowing must help, too). His pals Jack Lemmon and Bill Murray say he's a natural on the stage. Jacobsen was going into Manhattan on Tuesday evening to catch Lemmon in *Long Day's Journey into Night* and planned dinner one evening during Open Week with Murray. He knows every line from *Caddyshack*. One of his favorite books is the Zen-influenced *Golf in the Kingdom* by Michael Murphy, founder of the Esalen Institute in California. Jacobsen wants to make a movie version in which he plays the American protagonist who starts off hooking and slicing before he learns about the real game of golf from the wise Scottish pro Shivas Irons.

I once wrote about Jacobsen, "Maybe his real ambition is to be a great entertainer. A golfing career may just be the first act." I also asked, "Does a personality so generous with its energies best serve the promise of the player's golf ability?"

Look at many of the great pros and you'll doubt it—Hogan, Snead, Nelson, Watson, Kite, Nicklaus. It's a long list. But look at fun-loving Lee Trevino. Isn't he living proof that the double life can be pulled off? Not really, because beneath Trevino's fan-pleasing horseplay is a hard man. Off the golf course the public Merry Mex is a recluse who doesn't always turn the other cheek when dealing with fools.

When I asked him about that issue in connection with

another crowd favorite, Jacobsen, Trevino offered this anecdote: "I was five or six years on the tour before I realized that I
couldn't play around forever out here and stay on top. One
year at the World Series of Golf, I went out to the practice tee
early, took my radio and turned it up real loud. I didn't want
to hear any banter and questions—my game needed work.
Well, one guy stepped over the ropes and turned the radio
down! I asked him what the heck he was doing. He said he
wanted to ask me a question and I couldn't hear it.

"'That's right, pal,' I said. 'That's why I had the radio
turned up!'

"And if the guy doesn't understand this, I don't need him
as a friend or a fan."

Peter Jacobsen hadn't played Shinnecock Hills before
that Monday morning. On Sunday he walked the course
without hitting a shot. He likes to do that with a strange layout
because, he said, "every shot will be perfect. It gets me in a
good frame of mind."

And he was playing alone on Monday so he wouldn't be
distracted by the chatter of other pros. On the sixth hole, a
ferocious dogleg right with a long carry for the drive over
rough, Jacobsen and his caddie mulled the options off the tee,
in different winds. That day the gale was dead into the golfers.
His drive made the fairway with little room to spare. The
second shot on the par-four hole was a long iron or a fairway
wood, with a pond—the only water on the course—short and
right of the green. Jacobsen hit a long iron to the front collar.
Then he walked over to the rough and dropped a ball and
tried to hit a long iron out of that grass. The ball plunged into
the water. "I'll just have to wedge out if I miss the fairway," he
said. On the green he knocked a few putts from various

positions to various targets—likely pin positions when the tournament started.

Then he moved on to the seventh hole, the par three with the dangerously sloping green. With the wind coming from the right, Jacobsen noted that what the shot required was a left-to-right fade, into the wind, into the slant of the green. He put the ball pin high.

On the ninth tee, a dogleg left to the green up by the clubhouse, Jacobsen complained about the way the fairway accepted the tee shot: A long, accurate drive was in all likelihood "rewarded" by a hanging lie, a downhill stance for a long-iron shot to the elevated green. That's a virtually impossible shot; and while the pros understand that a golf course isn't meant to be fair, they're not amused by the "impossible for one, impossible for all" explanation. "It's funky," Jacobsen concluded about the new tee on nine.

Then, as we looked down the rolling carpet of fairway, the flagstick whipping far away on the green, the clubhouse silhouetted against the bright sky, he exclaimed, "This is golf! It's not about backswings and alignments." Right then I thought he was going to get esoteric and quote *Golf in the Kingdom* or something. Instead he said, "It's about getting the ball in the hole."

I was going to leave Jacobsen after the ninth hole. He had explained he liked to play alone his first time around but then spent most of the first nine conversing with me and Tom Doak, a friend of mine who had joined us along the way, a budding golf-course designer. Would Jacobsen have asked us to let him play the back nine in peace and quiet? I was wondering this when his caddie eased up and popped the question instead, explaining that he was afraid his boss was talking too much and not paying enough attention to his game and the course. I said the same notion had struck me, and farewells were exchanged. I hope Jacobsen had sent his man over to run us off.

I stalled around near the clubhouse to give him a head start on the back nine, then walked out on the tenth hole, a dramatic par four aimed to the east, bending slightly to the south. Beginning about 230 yards from the tee, the fairway dips down into a deep ravine, then runs up sharply to the wide, narrow green. The golfer has a decision: Hit the driver and hope to make it all the way to the flatland at the bottom of the ravine, or lay up short of the downslope with a long iron, thus assuring a flat lie but leaving a much longer approach shot. Any approach shot short of the green would stay short, perhaps even roll all the way down into the ravine, about twenty yards below the putting surface. On Monday, with the following breeze, players were hitting drives all the way down the slope, and wedges back up the hill.

I found big Andy Bean and a pro I didn't know playing the hole. I've always liked Bean's game, the purest industrial swing on the tour. With him *hulk* is a verb. He hulks down the fairway. He talks to anyone on the golf course. He talks to himself, especially after a weak shot: "How stupid can you be?" or "Isn't that pathetic? Can't hit the fairway with an iron!"

The twosome moved onto the eleventh hole, a little par three to a dangerous green that poses problems similar to those of the par-three seventh, but in reverse: Eleven slopes down from left to right, with two deep sand pits beneath the green; anything left slips down a slope, leaving a pitch from a bare lie to the downhill surface. When Bean's unknown playing partner holed that chip shot, the famous player turned to him and said with a wry smile, "You're not that good."

Bean then signaled his caddie for a few balls, dropped them at the top of the green, and lagged the putt down toward the pin in the center of the green. The balls rolled well past, one after the other. We would have been on that green thirty minutes if it had taken Bean that long to get one close. No pro walks away from a practice session on a losing note.

On the next tee, an elevated one, Bean socked his ball and then walked ahead, down the hillside, before his partner hit. He looked back and called out, "Can you hit one over my head, Smitty?" And Bean kept walking as Smith drove the ball right over his head. I wouldn't have walked down there. Pros do occasionally skim one off the tee—Trevino did so in the last round of the Open he won at Oak Hill, and so did North when he won at Cherry Hills, but Bean walked blithely into the night. (I was talking with Craig Stadler one year at the Westchester Country Club while he worked with a photographer setting up for a series of 5-iron shots. For the best lighting Stadler had to aim his shots over a busy walkway about one hundred yards away, but he hadn't noticed the jeopardy of the passersby until he was about to hit the first ball. Then he saw them, said calmly, "Ah, they're all right," and hit away.)

In *Caddyshack*, Chevy Chase has some fun with all the mental-side business when he instructs his young caddie: "Danny, I'm going to give you a little advice. There's a force in the universe that makes things happen and all you have to do is get in touch with it. Stop thinking. Let things happen and . . . be the ball . . . find your center . . . hear nothing . . . feel nothing."

Chase demonstrates by hitting a shot onto the green— blindfolded. "Try it, Danny." Danny ties up his eyes and addresses the shot. "Picture the shot . . . turn off the sound . . . be the ball." Danny hits it into the water.

A little later, Bill Murray gets his opportunity when he

tells a caddie about his experience carrying the bag for the Dalai Lama: "I'm on the first tee, I give him his driver, he hauls off and whacks one—big hitter, the Lama, long—into a 10,000-foot crevice right at the foot of this glacier. You know what the Lama says?

"'Gunga Lagunga. Gunga Lagunga.'"

Murray was impressed, but after the round the holy man tried to stiff him on the tip and Murray called him on it. Unabashed, the Lama announced that in lieu of cash his caddie would receive "total consciousness" on his deathbed.

"So I got that going for me," Murray concludes, "which is nice."

No one ever has fired hotter rounds of golf and strings of such rounds than Johnny Miller. In two- and three-week streaks in the mid-seventies, he played the game as well as it can be played, especially with his irons to the greens. The courses for those pyrotechnics weren't the hardest (the desert tracks in the West), but his marksmanship from the fairways was remarkable regardless, and in 1973 he also set the record (since tied) for low round in the U. S. Open, a 63 on the final day, passing everyone else at Oakmont—one of the most difficult courses in the world. In 1974 he won the first three tournaments of the season and eight all together, a feat not likely to be matched again. Then the following year he won the first two tournaments, at 24 and 25 under par. He has won twenty-three events on the tour and, in 1976, the British Open; three seconds in The Masters.

Miller is utterly straightforward, and has no sense whatsoever of public relations; ask the question and get an answer. A few weeks before the Open I called him at his home in Utah to see whether I could walk along on one of his practice rounds at Shinnecock Hills.

"Sure," he said. "What day?"

"Well, you name it. What's best for you?"

"It doesn't matter. I'm playing the course over the weekend, then I have an outing in New Jersey on Monday. Tuesday or Wednesday is fine. What's a good time?"

That's fairly remarkable cooperation from a pro, especially one of Miller's stature, and it wasn't calculated in the least, not coming from him. Of course, it didn't quite work out that way on Tuesday. Miller had been just as cooperative with George Peper, for whom Miller puts in some time as a Playing Editor, on *Golf Magazine*. Peper also had plans for Miller on Tuesday. We talked it over on the first tee, and I agreed to join them on the fairways in a couple of holes, giving Peper plenty of time for his questions.

As I stood around the sunny tee that morning with a hundred or so other fans, I noticed a man with a sack full of paintings of the pros. He had rendered them himself from photographs in the golf magazines, and he was getting autographs on his work. Miller glanced at his likeness—blond hair flying as he left his feet on a swing—and signed his name and thanked the man, an illustrator named Bill Atwell, a craggy-faced Tommy Bolt look-alike. He and I talked as Miller and Calvin Peete teed off and walked down the hill to the first fairway, George Peper in tow.

"I have something to compare these guys with," Atwell said, gesturing to the Open field at large. "I work one of the senior tour events. These guys out here don't give you anything."

I've worked at senior tour events, too, and I agree. The senior players—guys over fifty—do give a lot more of themselves to the fans. They're open and available for conversation, for the most part. They're also closer in age to many of the fans. For those professionals, the now-rich senior tour is a reprieve from a retirement that would not have left them nearly as flush as today's young players will be. Miller Barber, a regular on the senior tour, would be competing at Shinnecock Hills against golfers half his age. Thanks to the million dollars he's won at the senior events since 1981, Barber has passed up Arnold Palmer on the all-time money list.

I said good-bye to Bill Atwell and snuck up behind Miller and Peper on the second fairway, jumping the gun by a hole or two. When I related to Miller the conversation about young players versus their elders, he remarked, "By the time you learn how to handle the pressure of the people, you're over the hill!" That was in the old days. Now you're on the senior tour, having a good time, giving a good time, making money.

On that par-three second hole, Miller almost put his tee ball in the hole. "A finesse 2-iron," he announced, and that was a joke. He had swung the club as hard as he could, almost leaving his feet, the trademark of his swing (as Atwell knew when he painted his picture). Gary Player also leaves his feet on some swings, breaking a cardinal rule of the game: solid foundation and good balance—hallmarks, by the way, and not coincidentally, of Miller Barber. Here's the catch: Foundation and balance are required *at impact*, and Miller and Player are solid when it counts. What happens later doesn't matter. (Well, it does, of course, but the pros can handle it. Some can hit pretty good shots standing on one leg or sitting in a chair, as Seve Ballesteros demonstrates when he's showing off. My nephew Sam MacNaughton can nail them from his knees.)

As Miller and Peete walked from the third green to the fourth tee, their route took them close to the path from the sixth green to the seventh tee. "Johnny Miller!" A voice shouted out. "My hero!" Miller glanced over his shoulder, unhappy until he spotted the source of the trouble. It was Greg Norman, the unoriginal clone of the classic tour pro. Miller was "the original clone," as he puts it—the handsome blond golfer all the agents and marketeers pointed to while advising their clients, "Look like that."

On the fourth fairway Miller nodded toward Calvin Peete. "If I had his desire," he said, "I'd have won a bunch more."

Miller is one of the rare pros who will gladly grant that he doesn't always give a damn, that he has a little "quit" in him if a tournament is out of reach. Among the undriven golfers (and there are many, in this respect), he's the premier player thanks to his pure ball-striking talent. Miller also believes that he would have won more tournaments if he hadn't had so many children so soon after his marriage, six in ten years. "But so what," he asked rhetorically, and I thought about a remark Arnold Palmer made in the locker room at Shoal Creek near Birmingham, Alabama, prior to the PGA Championship in 1984. After Palmer was established as a superstar in the sixties, he plunged into myriad outside interests that must have cost him some tournaments. "So what," he asked. "I enjoyed all the other things, too."

Golf has never been Johnny Miller's whole life. Of course, he could afford to be undriven, thanks to a contract his agent made with Sears Roebuck in the early seventies. Miller's line of clothing had its own button on the cash register. The money set him up for life, as he acknowledges.

Jack Nicklaus never quits, and that's probably the biggest difference between his golf and Johnny Miller's, a difference not in the swing but very much in the *game*. When I was in Houston watching my nephew play, Jack Montgomery, the former pro, told me about a round he played with Nicklaus at the Colonial in Fort Worth in 1969.

"Nicklaus had nothing that day," Montgomery said. "He was all over the golf course—one he didn't like—but he kept grinding and grinding. And he shot a 69. That's Jack Nicklaus."

The other pros have concluded the same thing, but it's a relative point. While Miller concedes some deficiency in this regard, he also notes with pride that he "hung in" during his horrible slump in 1978–1979, when he lost control of his game entirely. And he was winless the year before that, so it was almost four years between victories in 1976 and 1980. Miller is undriven compared with Nicklaus, perhaps, but not compared with me.

As Miller walked the front nine, seeing Shinnecock Hills for the second time, he was "looking for red lights—while trying not to think negatively." When he said that, I thought about the shank he'd told me about. And I thought about a piece in one of the newspapers prior to The Masters two months earlier. Three or four pros were asked which shot on the back nine at Augusta National they considered the most dangerous. Nicklaus alone declined to answer, explaining that he might end up with that shot and wouldn't want in his mind the thought that it was the "most dangerous." That's Jack Nicklaus, too.

One red light Miller spotted was the back of the green on the fifth hole, which falls off drastically. He flipped a few balls into the rough in front of the green, a likely resting place for his second shot on the par five, and chipped from that position, demonstrating his brand-new stroke for chip shots—brand-new in this, his seventeenth year of tour golf. It was a one-speed execution, he said, like his sand-wedge stroke. The results were acceptable.

As he rolled a few putts toward imaginary holes, he said, "Caddies tend to underread putts." They don't read in enough break. That might be the case at the pro level, but in my experience local caddies are beyond compare. I have good eyes and have lined up putts that I was certain would break considerably in one direction, only to be told to play exactly the opposite break. The caddie was right, always. A putt has to be properly read and properly struck. Nothing else will do, and even then it often fails to fall in. But a putt never falls after it is misread but then mishit in accidental compensation for the misreading. This is perverse: Spike marks seem to kick the ball aside but never in.

"Pros judge a golf course by the pin positions," Miller offered as he studied the USGA's likely choices on that fifth green. Like many established players, Miller is getting involved in design, working in an advisory capacity with established, full-time architects. Jack Nicklaus has been designing courses for years, and he agrees with Miller. Nicklaus spends most of his time on an architecture job working on the greens. From the pros' demanding point of view, designing a green with four different and fair pin positions—one for each day of a tournament—is no easy accomplishment. The tour stops at some putt-putt layouts, and many top golfers—among them Nicklaus, Ballesteros, and Watson—tend to avoid these courses, such as the desert layouts on which Miller ran the tables. The great pros don't want a putting contest on flat surfaces, which gives the prize to whoever's hot for the week. Good greens with challenging pin placements guarantee a tougher time for all, and that's what the better players want, as well as the bad putters, who have a better chance of matching two putts against the field than of matching one-putt birdies. Miller was a good putter but now he's not, and he uses a weird model with a long handle that he presses against his chest for stability. Quite a few senior golfers are using that model, too. It's not a good sign when a player begins such experimentation; he's doubting his basic stroke and looking for peculiar help. Nevertheless, Miller said he could play this Shinnecock Hills course and play it well.

I wished him luck, waved good-bye to George Peper, and walked back to the practice tee. Peter Oosterhuis, a big Englishman who now lives in Dallas, was hitting shots with his short backswing. He had practiced early, played, and was now practicing again. His opinion of Shinnecock Hills? "It's more England than England," thereby affirming an opinion delivered by Nicklaus after a tune-up round played months before. Though I wasn't sure, it seemed they were saying that while Shinnecock Hills is rustic compared with Augusta National, it's refined by comparison to the true Scottish links. I'd make my own judgment on that score when I went overseas later in the summer.

At five o'clock Tuesday afternoon I had a choice: Nicklaus's interview in the press tent, or more golf on the practice tee and nearby holes. I chose the golf. Nicklaus has done thousands of interviews, saying the same things thousands of times. He does it beautifully and is usually gracious, although occasionally his boredom shows.

Guessing the winning score is a ritual all the top players are put through, and Nicklaus had already stated that he thought even-par 280 would win at Shinnecock Hills. When this pronouncement was mentioned during a practice round, one pro snorted, "Well, then, I guess there's no reason for me to shoot 279." It's not the only snide remark I've heard players make about Nicklaus, who can sound oracular in press conferences. But is that his fault, or ours?

In 1982 I spent a day with Nicklaus, flying on his leased jet from New Jersey to a layout he was designing in Banner Elk, North Carolina. He worked there for a few hours and then we flew on late in the day to West Palm Beach, where he lives. I learned more about him in those eight hours than I could have at a thousand press conferences.

I was doing a story on his work designing golf courses for *Connoisseur* magazine, not a golfing magazine, certainly, and not Nicklaus's normal market at all. Maybe that's why my request for the day-long interview was granted without much delay. I arrived early at Teterboro Airport in New Jersey and waited for him and his party to arrive from midtown Manhattan. Their limousine pulled onto the tarmac beside the airplane while I was talking with one of the pilots in the cockpit. We had never met formally, so I stepped back to the stairs and introduced myself to Nicklaus as he climbed up. His clear blue eyes greeted me frankly and evenly, which didn't surprise me. I knew he handled himself well in news conferences, and his work off the course requires meeting hundreds of people, some of whom want a piece of him but some of whom might be useful and maybe even interesting, and therefore to be handled with care. We settled down in the cabin with a couple of his assistants, including Bob Cupp, his main designer.

Everybody chatted and Nicklaus, a pilot, peered through the window and commented on some of the sleek jets at Teterboro (a facility for private planes), and explained how he became interested in design work. In the sixties he played a lot of exhibitions on bad golf courses all over the world. Robert Trent Jones's theories of "heroic" golf-course design had produced some good layouts, but in the wrong hands just as many, or more, bad ones—spurious copies that boasted a bountiful use of the land but lacked originality. In Nicklaus's parlance, "turf nurseries."

In the seventies, while playing the best golf of his career, he began his own design work in earnest. He didn't have any trouble breaking into the business. One of his first efforts was at the Harbour Town Golf Links, on Hilton Head Island, South Carolina, where he worked with the architect of record, Pete Dye, to build what is acknowledged as one of the best new courses in the world. This short, flavorful course on flat land doesn't pretend to be anything else, eighteen holes playable by the average golfer but challenging to the tour pros, who play the Sea Pines Heritage Classic there every spring. "Playability" for the handicap golfer would seem to be a prerequisite for a resort layout, but not necessarily. Some developers believe that traveling golfers want monster courses on which a high score becomes a boast, and every hole is a postcard home.

I asked Nicklaus to label his design theory—penal, strategic, or heroic?—and he grudgingly said strategic, but with elements of the other two, mostly heroic. He doesn't work with concepts, he said, but with the land, and a staff of top technical people. He acknowledged two tenets of his trade: the need for "relief" on a golf course, and his own visceral desire for the concave over the convex.

At all points, from every angle, the player will see relief on a Nicklaus golf course, abrupt changes in elevation and contrast. The lip of a bunker and the shadow it casts are such a change and in his opinion a small but vital one. Relief sets up the golf course, pleasing the eye and helping the golfer target his shot. "Concavity invites, convexity repels," he said. Nicklaus has turned down design jobs working with domelike land. He wants every hole to be either concave or to deceive the eye into believing that it is. The ultimate sin of convexity is a blind shot over a rise. There won't ever be one on a Nicklaus course. (The ninth hole at Shinnecock Hills comes close to being such a convex mistake, but the green is hollowed out of the hillside and presents itself as friendly terrain.)

After we took off from Teterboro, Nicklaus passed around a tray of fruit, and someone produced the pad of blueprints and sketches for the golf course we were flying to, the Elk River Club. I watched and listened as Nicklaus and Cupp discussed the progress, the problems that had come up, and the decisions that had to be made that afternoon. Nicklaus visits his golf courses once or twice before they get going and once, maybe twice, during the heavy construction, and then several times if necessary when the final work on the greens and bunkers is completed. "Ninety percent of a golf course is underground," Nicklaus said. "I work with the other ten percent."

On the airplane I thought I'd been invited to a performance staged for my benefit, demonstrating Nicklaus's grasp of the details of the job, assuring me that he wasn't merely a figurehead designer hired for his name alone. He certainly was hired for his designer-label name, in part, and he wouldn't have bothered to deny that it would sell residential lots or club memberships or high green fees. But Nicklaus wanted me to understand that he was also the designer of the golf course. He knew what he was talking about, I was convinced of that, but the staff meeting on the plane struck me as just another news conference, mainly.

The landing strip we aimed for was adjacent to the mucked-up golf course (lots of rain; I'd been warned to bring boots), and Nicklaus studied the mud as we coasted in. The owners of the club greeted us and we joined them and local residents for a quick lunch in the temporary headquarters. Then Nicklaus, Cupp, the owners, and I donned our boots and hit the course.

This was a different Jack Nicklaus. He clearly enjoyed tromping around in the mud while studying the construction and dickering with Bob Cupp and, occasionally, the owner. A couple of holes on the back nine weren't working out as expected. Only so much can be gleaned from topographical maps; much more is revealed once a few trees are cut down and the fairways established. I was brought into the discussions as just another opinion. My role as a recording journalist was beside the point. Nicklaus's role as the celebrity was dropped, and I had the distinct impression that he was much happier with this arrangement.

That afternoon I decided Nicklaus merely tolerates the

public relations part of his job, and is perfectly aware of how dehumanizing it is—both for master and disciples. Some of the pros seem to enjoy putting on the no-face air of the superstar, which then becomes their identity both on and off the course. Nicklaus, I believe, looks forward to shedding it.

We had fun on the Elk River course. When Nicklaus lit his first cigarette of the day, I frowned and exclaimed playfully, "My wife will be shocked!"

"I know," Nicklaus replied, almost sheepishly. He told me the story about how he quit smoking on the golf course after he saw a tape of himself taking a drag during a tournament and realized how unsightly it was. He quit—publicly. I take this temperence as another example of his self-control: The golf course would logically be where he would want a cigarette the most.

Work completed, we boarded the waiting jet and flew to West Palm Beach. Flying was the main subject of conversation between naps (Nicklaus tries to doze during flights), although he did urge me to see his Desert Highlands layout near Phoenix. He was frankly proud of that flat piece of land wrapped around Pinnacle Peak. The concept incorporates turf areas from the residential development into the golf course, and these "intersections" are the green target areas of the fairways. Sand areas at the edges of almost all the target areas spread out into the desert. Bands of the desert sweep into the golf course and out again into the development. Elaborate internal drainage protects the desert from the irrigation water used on the course. Hundreds of native cacti were planted and transplanted. "The vegetation," Nicklaus said, "enhances the design and disguises the golf course. You're going to hear a lot about that one. It's a really neat course. Even some people from the Sierra Club have liked our ideas!" In 1983 and '84, Desert Highlands was the first host course for what has become the annual Thanksgiving Weekend Skins game, a popular TV production featuring, those two years, Nicklaus, Palmer, Player, and Watson.

At the airport in West Palm we were met by a house-keeper driving the Nicklaus family station wagon. Nicklaus made certain my accommodations for the night were in order and invited me to drop by his house the next day to see his extensive nursery of grasses, trees, plants, and flowers. He couldn't be there, he said, but a scholarship student in hor-ticulture would show me around. Then we said good-bye.

Tom Watson has a commendable method for dealing with news conferences and the thousands of more informal ques-tions he fields every season. "I just answer every question as honestly as I can," he told me once.

Memoirs of Hadrian, by the contemporary French au-thor Marguerite Yourcenar, has this passage in which the Roman emperor describes his strategy for getting through the tedium of his official duties:

> To give oneself totally to each person throughout the duration of a hearing; to reduce the world for a moment to this banker, that veteran, or that widow; to accord to these individuals, each so different though each confined naturally within the narrow limits of a type, all the polite attention which at the best moments one gives to oneself, and to see them, almost every time, make use of this opportunity to swell themselves out like a frog in the fable; furthermore, to devote seriously a few moments to thinking about their business or their problem.

After Thursday's first round, with all of the high scores induced mainly by the weather, any player standing at 75 or better was in fine shape for the next three rounds. A 77 or 78 was not a bad score if it would be followed quickly by a much better one. At the 1985 Masters, Curtis Strange shot an 80 in the first round, twelve shots behind the leader, but he came back with 65-68-71 and almost won the tournament. In fact, he sort of lost the tournament in the last holes, but it was nevertheless courageous golf after that first round. Strange was hot all that year, winning three tournaments and leading the money list. The 80 was the fluke, not the comeback.

The pros often state that major championships don't really begin until the final nine holes on Sunday. The preceding 63 holes are just preliminary positioning. In tennis, lose the first round and you're out of the event. In golf, you have another chance; then if you make the cut, you have two more. An irony of golf decrees that the terrible shot does not carry over if a great shot makes up for it and saves par, but the terrible shot that isn't rescued, that causes a triple bogey on the second hole on Thursday, is a monkey on the player's back for the rest of the tournament. In tennis, lose the game or the set and forget it; start clean with the next one. With the cumulative scoring of golf you never start over, and that can work for you, if you shot a 61 in the first round, or against you, if an 80.

In the old days, much competitive golf was match play, wherein the low score wins the hole and the match is determined by the winner of the most holes, not the lowest cumulative score. A golfer hopelessly out of one hole simply picks up and concedes it—down one hole, not two or three or four shots. Match play, like par, is a leveler. It's a different game entirely, and most friendly golf games are match play of one sort or another; but it's no good for the pros. Too many top players lose a match in the early rounds and aren't around for the television broadcasts. For a few years the Tucson Open was a match play format, but that experiment was dropped for 1987 and thereafter. The semifinalists in 1985 were Mac O'Grady, Bob Tway, Jack Renner, and Jim Thorpe, who won. In 1986 the semifinalists were Scott Simpson, Phil Blackmar, Ken Green, and Thorpe, again the winner. Bobby Jones wrote, "Match play can be a pretty game and exciting, but it can never exert the relentless pressure of the card and pencil."

After Thursday's round at Shinnecock Hills the card and pencil had decreed this leader board:

E	Bob Tway	Lanny Wadkins
+1	Greg Norman	Lee Trevino
+2	Kenny Knox	Tom Kite
	Tom Watson	T. M. Chen
	Denis Watson	others
	David Frost	+5 Mac O'Grady
	Rick Fehr	Ray Floyd
	Tommy Nakajima	Hal Sutton
+3	Jody Mudd	Fuzzy Zoeller
	Gary Koch	Seve Ballesteros
	Bob Lohr	Scott Verplank
+4	Craig Stadler	others
	Bernhard Langer	+6 Ben Crenshaw

	Peter Jacobsen		others
	Johnny Miller	+8	Sandy Lyle
	Andy Bean		others
	T. C. Chen	+9	Andy North
	others		others
+7	Calvin Peete	+10	Miller Barber
	Hale Irwin		others
	Jack Nicklaus	+15	Bob Eaks
	Thomas Cleaver		Jack Renner (withdrew)
	Wayne Smith		others

On Friday morning the winds had switched almost one hundred eighty degrees from the Nor'easterly blow of the first round, and were breezing away from the west. The sun was shining. Everyone was happy. I chose to begin the day with the sharp pairing of Johnny Miller, Seve Ballesteros, and Bill Rogers, a top player in the early eighties (winner of the British Open) who has since lost interest in the pro game. He's thirty-five years old.

On the sixth hole, the long par four playing into the wind, Miller hit a beautiful fairway wood to the green, twenty feet from the hole. Ballesteros drilled a long-iron even closer. Rogers missed the green. Miller then left his putt short and glared at the ball. And there you have it. Miller can't putt anymore, even with his new blade wedged against his chest. After missing the birdie he walked off to the side of the green and stared back down the fairway. Was tension building for Miller? No, too early in the tournament. Anger incapacitating? I doubted it; he's a veteran and knows his problem. Doubt gnawing? That I believed. When you start fooling around with weird putters, doubt is never far away. Rare is the pro golfer who loses his putting stroke only to recover it years later. I can't think of one case, and Tom Watson is going to have to win some tournaments to prove me wrong. Nicklaus's great putting at The Masters in 1986 doesn't count in this regard, because it's probable that his incredible putts for the victory were sheer, unadulterated magic, a gift from the gods of golf, who aren't crazy after all. There are many instances of a one-week return to form, but a fundamental recovery of the touch of one's youth? Doubt gnawed in Miller's mind with good reason. I imagine Watson is wondering, too, despite his pronouncements to the contrary.

Ballesteros sank his putt. As the ball dropped, I was standing next to John Andrisani, the main instruction editor at *Golf Magazine* and the coauthor of Ballesteros's auto-biographical instruction book, so I asked him what he thought had happened at The Masters, on the ill-fated shot into the water on the fifteenth hole. Ballesteros, he said, was inde-cisive about what club to hit, wavering between a smooth four-iron and a hard five, and wasn't certain even after he finally chose the four-iron. Some doubt had lingered, as proved by the poor swing. The mind, the body, the dichotomy: The instructions from the mind must be perfectly clear in order for the body to have a chance of making the swing.

I also believe Ballesteros might have been a little spooked by the thunderous cheers for Nicklaus that were rolling across Augusta National. Ballesteros has said he doesn't believe he gets his due from American fans, and he's right. The best player in the game over the past three years, he was playing at Shinnecock Hills on Friday in relative privacy, with a gallery of, at most, a hundred and fifty. American fans like Seve, but he's no hero. A mark against him is his admission that he doesn't particularly enjoy playing over here, though he main-tains an admirable bonhomie, generally smiling and friendly. On the last holes at The Masters, when he knew he'd blown it, he played with remarkable equanimity, almost cheer-fulness, so much so that I wondered how he pulled it off. Another mark against him, perhaps, is his lack of playing time in the States. He was semi-banned from the tour by commissioner Deane Beman following a dispute over an alleged agreement regarding how many tournaments Ballesteros would play in America.

How, then, could American fans welcome him as the conquering hero? Conquering is the key word. American hegemony in the game is long gone. Ballesteros, Bernhard Langer, and Greg Norman—three of the top six golfers in the world by any measurement—are not Americans. A decade ago there was one, South Africa's Gary Player. And there are now any number of European, Asian, and South African or Zimbabwean golfers who are just as good as the rank and file of American pros. T. C. Chen, the virtual unknown from Taiwan, almost won last year's Open. The European Tour is the fastest growing in the world, thanks in large measure to the tidy under-the-table appearance fees for the top players. Ballesteros receives about thirty thousand dollars just to show up at a European event. Such fees are forbidden on the PGA Tour, and apparently this rule is observed, although some senior golfers assert that a certain top player on that tour doesn't appear unless a lucrative corporate outing is set up in conjunction with the event—in effect, an appearance fee. Foreign competition in golf isn't as pronounced as it is in professional tennis, where Americans are frankly on the wane and Europeans dominate, but it could be heading there. What if the Czechs should take up golf next?

Andrisani mentioned another possible factor on Ballesteros's fifteenth hole, a point I, too, had noticed: overconfidence. On the thirteenth hole, he had turned to his caddie and confidently patted him on the back after a fine second shot—a gesture of victory, almost, much more fitting on the eighteenth fairway than on the thirteenth. If the real golf tournament hadn't even started until the midway point in that final round, then it wasn't even half over—way too early even to think about winning. But two holes later, Ballesteros could begin to think about losing.

Ballesteros and Miller were followed onto the sixth hole at Shinnecock Hills by Dave Eichelberger, the journeyman with a new swing that hadn't produced much on Thursday, when he cobbled together an 80. But Eichelberger struck a beautiful iron to the green and the ball almost rolled in the hole for an eagle. This six-inch birdie put him one under for the round. Playing with Eichelberger was the sober pro Joe Inman, the consummate journeyman: one victory in thirteen years on the tour, and that, probably, is all she wrote. Inman doesn't hit the ball far enough. Bigger, stronger golfers and advanced equipment and balls have utterly changed the game in the last decade.

There have always been powerful hitters—Sam Snead put the ball a long way out there—but now there are many powerful hitters, some of whom also have all the rest of the game. A Greg Norman has a tremendous advantage over a Joe Inman. Inman would have to play his absolute best golf for seventy-two holes and Norman some of his worst for the two players to finish close. That's a new, hard fact of life on the tour for the shorter hitters, who are now an endangered species. Calvin Peete, the short hitter with superior accuracy, acknowledges that he's the exception to the rule and perhaps the last of the breed. And what is this difference between short and long? On average, only twenty yards in the air with the driver. However, the longer hitter can move it even farther if a hole makes it worthwhile, and he also hits his irons farther, so he might be coming into the green with an eight-iron instead of a five. The short man has to be superaccurate to compensate for this disadvantage. Inman says that accuracy and a good short game will overcome anything, but that's not quite true. They won't overcome the longer hitter who's also accurate and has a good short game.

Short hitter Jim Simons was more frank when he asked me, "How long will I be able to keep it up?"

If the rest of the greens at Shinnecock Hills were playing like the sixth green, the pros were going to have an enjoyable round of golf on Friday, even with the wind. After Thursday's rain the green was soft. The balls hit and held. Target practice, the pros say. Johnny Miller bristles when it's pointed out that his record-setting 63 at Oakmont to win the Open in 1973 was accomplished on rain-softened greens. Oakmont greens are usually hard and difficult to hold, but that day the pros were firing right at the flags.

Amateurs usually think only about how fast the greens are putting, because we don't fly them with the second shot anyway. The pros do, and they're just as concerned with how firm the greens are. Are they soft enough to accept the approach shot or, like concrete, do they reject it? If the ball hits on but bounces over, the pros may complain that they're playing funny golf. The good shot onto the green isn't rewarded, in that view, and some pros don't want to alter their approach and run the ball onto the putting surface.

Following Eichelberger and Inman into six was Bobby Clampett. What a story Clampett is, or was. His agents at the International Management Group (run by Mark McCormack, the superagent who wrote, or put his name to, *What They Don't Teach You at Harvard Business School*) established him as a superstar before he teed up his first ball as a pro in 1981. Clampett was a great college player, and he was smart and articulate with the curly-haired good looks of a teenage pinup. He couldn't miss as a player or as an advertising medium. His golf bag immediately became a billboard.

In his first year on the tour, Clampett lived up to his

reputation, finishing fourteenth on the money list with a lot of good tournaments. He led the British Open after the first round and astonished the writers with hypertechnical explanations of his game and his power—the bones and joints as levers and pistons, all of it the theory of *The Golfing Machine*, an instruction book in vogue at the time. He flagged a little the following year, but won the last event of the season. Then he got worse. Then he got terrible. In 1985, he had only two top-ten finishes in thirty tournaments. Needless to say, Clampett has been searching ever since for an alternative to the daunting strictures of *The Golfing Machine*.

His saga is cited by onlookers and fellow pros as a textbook example of the dangers of early, unearned success, and the pitfalls of hype. Clampett made a lot of money without having to perform. Presumably most of those endorsement contracts have now lapsed and he'll have to play good golf to earn them back again. What if Jack Nicklaus had come along with a glamour-boy image in an easy-money era? Would he have succumbed to the lures of premature fame and fortune? A poll of golf writers and officials would conclude in the negative. That's how strongly the golf world feels about Nicklaus's rock-solid character and great golf game. At any rate, agents are now more likely to take it slow with a hot prospect, bearing in mind the Clampett burn-out syndrome (which, by the way, he denies).

I shifted over to the back nine and found Lee Trevino on the par-five sixteenth hole. After he sank a 12 footer for birdie, he turned toward the bleachers on the east side of the green and peppered the delighted crowd with his pistol-firing routine. The fans love it; the pros less so. The pro who most irritated his peers with such shenanigans was Chi Chi Rodriguez, who now plays with the seniors. Rodriguez's favorite routine after sinking a birdie is to play the fencer with drawn sword. Touché! Then he sheathes his putter in triumph. If a fellow player is in the wrong mood, Chi Chi's wide range of distractions will burn him up. Dave Hill, who was easily burned up, wanted to fight Rodriguez, a good friend at all other times, after one episode back in 1970 at the Kemper Open outside Washington, D. C. Hill recounts the classic story in his book. During the last day, he was in contention and Chi Chi wasn't, and they were playing thirty-six holes together. On the fifth hole of the day's second round, Rodriguez sank a birdie and plopped his straw hat over the hole, to keep the ball from flying out before the birdie was recorded. Very funny, in the judgment of the fans. On the next tee, he auditioned his Puerto Rican vaudeville routine— jokes about rice and beans, mostly. Hill waited for the guffaws to die down. When they didn't, he hit anyway—and drove way left. While Hill was working on his approach shot out of the rough, Rodriguez was still clowning around, out of sight but not out of hearing. On the green, more antics, and Hill asked Rodriguez to keep it down, please, for the rest of the round. Chi Chi and the crowd turned against him then, and on the next hole Chi Chi informed an official he wouldn't play with Hill; the official told him he had to. Hill then birdied two holes, something else happened, and Rodriguez wanted to start a fight. Hill asked him for a nine-hole rain check, then triple bogeyed the eleventh hole, missed a putt to tie for the tournament on the eighteenth green, and went to Chi Chi's locker ready for blood. Bystanders intervened, and Hill says the matter never again came up between the two friends. Rodriguez still clowns around, but I don't imagine the seniors mind at all. His instructional clinic featuring trick shots and comedy is first-rate, and he has a well-deserved reputation for charitable acts.

Finally Jack Nicklaus arrived at the sixteenth hole. The fans had been waiting. From the vantage point of the bleachers beside the green, you couldn't quite see the tee from the lower stands. The golfers popped over a low rise in the fairway just about where their drives had landed. The fans had consulted their pairing sheets for the round and knew who was coming next.

"Which one is he?"

"Is he in the fairway?"

"What's his score?"

Nicklaus was nine over par for the tournament, two over for the round. And there he was in the fairway: good drive. Paired with him were Larry Nelson, the 1983 Open champ, and John Mahaffey, who has barely missed winning the Open a couple of times.

Sixteen is one of the few par fives that even the longest pro couldn't reach in two shots, so they didn't even try. Whereas the amateur wants to get as close as possible to the green at all times, the pros often prefer to lay back if they can't make it. Nicklaus's second shot soared up in the distance and descended onto the fairway about a hundred yards from the green. From a hundred yards, he could put maximum spin on the wedge shot for maximum bite (and maximum control). Besides, the fairway of sixteen was a little wider at that point.

Nicklaus wedged to twelve feet on his third shot. As he prepared to putt, every head was turned his way, every mouth was shut. The huge bleachers set up on the eighteenth green faced away from sixteen, but as many people as could pack onto the top rows of those stands turned in his direction. A couple of hills along the eighteenth fairway offered minimal views, and they, too, were packed. Three sides of the seventeenth tee were filled. And of course both sides of the sixteenth fairway, extending back fifty yards, were three-deep with his fans, and the green itself was five-deep.

Nicklaus's score was posted on several scoreboards, so the fans knew he had an acceptable round going on Friday, if a barely contending position in the tournament. However, he was six shots out of the lead at The Masters before he birdied the ninth hole on Sunday, and he won there. Sink this putt and you're eight over for the Open, Jack; only eight behind. That's what the fans were thinking. Hold that position going into the third round and you're fine. "If he gets in the hunt, they'll hear footsteps," was the wisdom on *Golf Digest's* pre-tournament tout sheet that listed Nicklaus as a 25-to-1 long shot, and that much was true. (No odds were given on Nicklaus before The Masters, where he wasn't supposed to be a factor.)

He crouched over the putt with the MacGregor Response Z-T (for zero-twist) putter made famous at The Masters, and eyed the line twice. Nelson and Mahaffey watched intently as Nicklaus rolled the ball into the cup. All together, fifteen seconds. In the old days he stood over putts for half a minute or more, and pros marveled at his concentration. (In a famous story he looked up after sinking a putt and inquired, "Was that a real dog?" That kind of story you don't want to research for truthfulness, so I haven't.) Some people predicted Nicklaus's nerves would go because of those long meditations, but they haven't. He's just not as good a putter now, and that's fair enough. Quick math counts at least sixty thousand putts he has struck in tournament play, and probably twice as many in practice and other rounds. And he worked on every one.

After this particular birdie, the thousands who had watched anxiously and silently now erupted with joy, and Nicklaus acknowledged the wild cheers in his relatively modest way. The jig he danced on the sixteenth green at Augusta National in 1975, after sinking a 40 footer, was so far out of character that it entered the realm of anecdote. Don't wait for the Golden Bear to toss his cap over the hole or sheathe his putter. These days, however, he does seem to offer an explanation for every missed putt. Too many years in front of the camera, perhaps; too much lost privacy.

All eyes now turned toward the seventeenth hole, a par three. Nicklaus hit his iron short of the green, and right. The crowd groaned, and again, louder, when he bogeyed the hole. Plus nine again and he finished with that score. Surrounded by well-wishers, he walked up the hill to the scoring tent.

For Friday afternoon's play I chose to follow Mac O'Grady. Starting the day at plus five, he was even par for the round through nine holes, perfectly good shape this early in the tournament. I joined his wife, Fumiko, in the small gallery on the tenth tee.

O'Grady is a colorful, outspoken pro with an unusual life story, and he has always received a lot of attention from writers who consider many of the other players, especially the younger ones, dull beyond belief, which in some cases they are, especially when dealing with the press. That's the start of a vicious circle. The other pros resented O'Grady's publicity—Hubert Green, a former U. S. Open champion, asked, "What has he ever done?"—and didn't understand the man himself whatsoever. He was not, by any stretch, one of them. After failing to qualify for the tour seventeen times (the record), he was an unusually old thirty-one when he finally qualified in 1982. His wife is Japanese. At one time he advocated the arcane doctrines of *The Golfing Machine*. He now follows a strict regimen for conditioning, which included running marathons in earlier years, and lists "modern times, sciences, and history" as his special interests (while most players cite fishing and sports). He was easily the most unusual character to hit the pro tour in a long time—the most unusual with a chance to win, at least. *Sports Illustrated* ran a major profile—about which he became so angry that he wouldn't talk with any reporter at all, on the record, for months. I was present while he calmly lectured an *SI* writer (not the author of the piece) for fully half an hour at a tournament in Hartford, Connecticut, in 1984, detailing dozens of alleged mistakes.

And then there is O'Grady's bitter dispute with Deane Beman, the commissioner of the PGA Tour. At the time of the U. S. Open, O'Grady was under threat of suspension for alleged violations of tour regulations regarding civil behavior. After Beman had withheld part of his paycheck as a means of collecting a fine, O'Grady publicly referred to the commissioner as a thief. After Shinnecock and after he won his first tour event—at Hartford—O'Grady lost his case on appeal and was suspended for six weeks.

The dispute was nasty and protracted, and the rest of the pros, conservative men for the most part, just wanted it to go away, even though many of them privately disagreed with some of Beman's policies. Tournament purses in the last decade have risen dramatically, and some of that largesse must be credited to Beman's entrepreneurial skill in rounding up corporate sponsorships (including one with Vantage cigarettes, which O'Grady and a couple other players criticized). As a group, the pros were concerned about the public relations problems that might follow from O'Grady's charges, even if they were justified.

I first met Mac shortly after I started writing about golf, right when he joined the tour. I read a profile of him in the *Los Angeles Times* (he grew up in southern California) and figured he was worthy of a national piece (offbeat if not famous). The saga of the iconoclastic golf pro who wouldn't quit trying was our most popular profile in many years, and the magazine received a record number of letters.

O'Grady didn't play very well in 1983 or '84, but in 1985 he soared to twentieth on the money list, with winnings of $223,000. When the quarrel with Beman became public knowledge, his celebrity increased. Some kids at Shinnecock Hills wore T-shirts proclaiming MAC O'GRADY RULES.

He doesn't shirk from this publicity. I had joined him for dinner on the Tuesday night before the tournament, along with his wife, his lawyer from San Diego, and a couple of golf equipment representatives. Mac boasted to a passing sports-writer—from *The New York Times*, no less—that he was going to win the U. S. Open. Everyone who knows the game, including the pros, agreed that O'Grady was due to win soon, but I doubted he could pull it off at Shinnecock Hills, his first Open. He's a different bird entirely, the rare pro whose mind and conversation tend toward abstraction and the abstruse, with flights of the imagination that have left me wondering what in the world he was talking about, and wondering whether he knew, for that matter. Mac's mind is a juggernaut. Most great golfers, most pros, are rooted in the here and now, and that's good for their games—one shot at a time; the previous shot is ancient history and the next one is still light years away. That's the best way for a golfer to look at things, and I had no sense that O'Grady had achieved this stolid groundedness, or was likely to acquire it suddenly in the national championship. He's a complex individual, to put it mildly. So is Ben Crenshaw, in his way, and that doesn't help him on the golf course. And Seve Ballesteros? Spontaneity and creativity have been known to backfire on the golf course. Jack Nicklaus is perfect for the game: impermeable to doubt, vacillation, and complication.

On the other hand, O'Grady does have one of the most

simple, solid swings on the tour, is a great ball striker, and hits the ball a mile although he's not a big man. If his putting came around on any given week, he could win, and win going away.

He doesn't practice much, at least not on the driving range. Instead, he swings in front of a mirror in his hotel room and works on the most recent mechanics he's picked up from various sources, now that he has disowned the formulations of *The Golfing Machine*. He swings right-handed and putts left-handed (but so does my father). With a little practice, O'Grady (but not my father) can switch it around and still play par golf.

On the practice tee on Tuesday, he was joking around with Lee Trevino and took his right-hander's metal driver, turned it over so that the clubhead was aimed straight down, swung left-handed, and socked a credible drive about 230 yards. The crowd cheered and the cameras clicked. Standing in the parking lot of his motel in Sag Harbor that evening before dinner, he hit a series of left-handed drives in the general direction of a cow out of range in an adjacent field. His lawyer, who has played in some pro events in Asia, hit regular drives with authority. I swung the club idly—no balls—and O'Grady said I had a pretty good looking swing.

This is how his back nine went on Friday:

10: Iron off the tee into the left rough. Barely over the green with approach iron (a quick discussion with his caddie about that!). Delicate chip almost in the hole. Par.

11: On a little par three that he admits scared him, a mid-iron plugged in the bunker short of the green. Impossible explosion into tall grass greenside. Another good chip and putt, but a bogey nonetheless.

12: Long drive in fairway. Iron to five feet. Missed putt. Par.

13: Perfect drive. Iron to eight feet. Missed putt. Par.

14: Drive in the right rough, could have been in trees

but caught a break. Iron to fifteen feet. Putt just fell in. Birdie.

15: Long drive dead center on the short par four. Wedge almost knocked down the flag but sucked back twenty feet. Angry, missed the putt. Par.

16: Drive dead center. Fairway wood to greenside bunker (one of the few golfers who even tried to reach the green in two). Good explosion to two feet. Birdie.

17: Pin high, twenty-plus feet. Missed putt. Par.

18: Fairway. Fourteen feet. Missed putt. Par.

The nine holes took about two hours, but the action is completely described by this short narrative. That's all that happens in golf, according to the scorecard, but it's everything else that happens in the meantime, the surge and draw of emotions, that makes golf worth playing or watching. O'Grady was riled after the bogey on the eleventh hole and stayed that way until the birdie on fourteen, which comforted him a little, but then got angry again when his wedge sucked so far back on fifteen, then the birdie on sixteen allowed him a relatively contented finish. He had said he would win the tournament and now, halfway through, he had a chance to do so. Four over par, he was one of the leaders, so he was invited to the press tent and I tagged along.

The announcement of his interview was made over the loudspeaker inside the cavernous tent, and about two dozen writers and the idly curious headed for the screened-off area that served as the official interview room. At one end were a table and several chairs. After he was introduced, O'Grady gave a brief rundown of his round—very much like my description, with a few comments thrown in—and then launched into a monologue about the spirit of America and dreams that never come true but sometimes do. After five minutes, writers began to leave. They couldn't use any of this material for quotes and, to be perfectly honest, O'Grady was just rambling. This wasn't his first official press interview, but there hadn't been many and, as I've said, Mac's mind is a juggernaut.

About eight guys were left when he finished, and a few called out questions: "About that wedge, Mac . . ." Then the interview was declared over and everyone surged forward for the informal session. Many writers don't want to participate in the more public session, from which they won't get anything exclusive. They want to ask their questions in the smaller group, without microphones. In this instance, they wanted O'Grady to talk about their chief interest, his dispute with Deane Beman.

Meanwhile, I studied the leader board. The best rounds on Friday were two-under-par 68s by Norman, Trevino, Floyd, and Payne Stewart. No surprises there. Lanny Wadkins's brother Bobby had a 69, along with O'Grady, while Lanny and Denis Watson had 70s, along with Bernhard Langer. Tom Watson had a 71. First-round leader Bob Tway had a 73.

The cut was set at ten-over-par 150, and Calvin Peete, Dave Eichelberger, and Andy North barely made it. Fuzzy Zoeller and Jack Nicklaus had one stroke to spare. At 148 were Ballesteros, Miller, T. C. Chen, Peter Jacobsen, Tom Kite, and Andy Bean. Of the seventy golfers who qualified for the final two rounds, only half a dozen were not touring pros of some accomplishment and only one—Sam Randolph—was an amateur. As always, some well-known golfers didn't make the cut, including John Mahaffey, Bobby Clampett, Curtis Strange, Dan Pohl, Jim Thorpe, George Burns, Bill Rogers, and two-time Open winner Hale Irwin.

Also missing the cut were first-off-the-tee Bob Eaks, Thomas Cleaver, and Wayne Smith. On Friday, Eaks shot an 86, the worst round of the day, and one more blow than on Thursday. His two-day total in the tournament, 171, was

thirty-two shots behind Greg Norman's leading score of 139.
The leaderboard for the championship, after two rounds:

−1	Norman		Langer
+2	Trevino		Stewart
+3	Watson, D.		Frost
	Floyd		O'Grady
	Tway	+5	Ben Crenshaw
	Watson, T.		Craig Stadler
+4	Wadkins, L.		Mark McCumber
	Wadkins, B.		Hal Sutton
	Nakajima		

Saturday was the weather we'd been waiting for—partly
cloudy, warm, with a stiff, southwesterly breeze, the prevailing one Shinnecock Hills had been designed for. Now the
USGA and the club members and the pros would find out how
well the grand old course would stand up to the challenge.
Thursday had been an unfair test, and nobody broke par. On
Friday eight players broke par (including Danny Edwards,
with a 69 to go with his opening-round 83, missing the cut;
and Joey Sindelar, with a course-record 66, to go with his first-
round 81, and he made the cut), and eleven others matched
par. That was a good showing in the westerly breeze on soft
greens. On Saturday the greens would be firmer.

For the last two days of the Open, the golfers are paired
in twosomes, not threesomes, and they play in reverse order
of their score for the tournament: highest scores first, leaders
last. Bradford Greer and Greg Powers teed off at 9:24 A.M.
Thirty-four groups later, the last twosome of Lee Trevino and
Greg Norman would depart down the hill at 2:30, right on
time for the beginning of the ABC broadcast.

By 10:45 the first fairway was lined almost tee to green.
Nicklaus was playing with the controversial David Ogrin, who

had published a diary about his rookie season that included some harsh remarks about his peers. That's not done.

Both golfers were ten strokes behind Norman. Nicklaus would have to shoot a round in the mid-60s on Saturday to push himself back into real contention (Ogrin, too, but who really cared?). He drove the first fairway, hit his iron to the middle of the green, and two putted for a routine par. On the long second hole, he put his tee shot into the bunker. I was standing in the gallery packed behind the green. "Jack," someone muttered, "you don't par this hole, you don't get past us. You'd better do it."

Partly this was New York pushiness, partly the unique attitude the fans have toward Nicklaus (and before him, toward Palmer). They own their hero. He plays golf *for* them. As it happened, Nicklaus exploded beautifully from the sand and emerged from the bunker with his hands high. The crowd, most of them aware that the short game is not his strength, roared with relief. The demanding fan said, "Thank you, Jack." Then everyone roared again when Nicklaus sank the par putt, and they let the Golden Bear pass on to the third hole. He parred it. He bogeyed four.

I veered from Nicklaus just in time to catch defending champion Andy North, playing the par-three seventh, eleven strokes behind Norman. No one has successfully defended an Open championship since Ben Hogan in 1951 (Nicklaus defended successfully at The Masters twenty years ago, and Watson at the British Open in 1983).

An amazing shot. North shanked his iron into the third fairway, at least fifty yards right of his target. Johnny Miller had told me about his shank, and I'd seen Billy Casper shank one on television, but North's shank witnessed in person—well, I'll admit I felt a little better about my own embarrassments. As he walked over to the ball, North seemed less perturbed than the gallery.

"Imagine," someone growled, "he won this tournament!"
"Twice!" a friend added, angrily.

Then North lofted a wonderful recovery shot up over the ridge and onto the green sloping away from him, and sank the short putt for par. It goes without saying that no one in the peanut gallery could've managed that.

Hard-working David Eichelberger was paired with big, burly Mark Calcavecchia, and I caught up with them on the ninth hole. Calcavecchia takes an earth-shattering wallop at the ball, especially with the driver. I believe this young pro swings harder than anyone on the tour. His swing is a far cry from the classic style that emphasizes timing and tempo, but his drive goes a mile, and on the ninth hole, at least, it landed in the fairway. Eichelberger set up for his shot on that tee. He's a fiddler, and repositioned his feet five times, each adjustment accompanied by a series of appraising glances down the fairway. He finally ended up very closed to the target—and snapped a wicked hook into the left rough, and very short. As everyone else walked off the tee, he retired to the side to manipulate his grip, which apparently had betrayed him. For his next shot from the very high grass, Eichelberger tried a 3-wood, and the ball sailed toward the equally high grass on the other side of the fairway.

"Fore right!" he yelled. Army golf. Eichelberger wasn't going to win any prizes this week.

I peeled off toward the first tee, where Johnny Miller and Seve Ballesteros were paired together, as they had been on Friday. Again they departed with a sparse gallery. Miller was gorgeous in pink and turquoise, Ballesteros in green and white. Nine strokes behind Norman, neither man was in any position to win. Then Ballesteros birdied the first, fifth, sixth, and eighth holes to gain four strokes on par, and he could have birdied several others after close iron approaches, but missed the putts. If he kept up this pace on the back nine, he'd be in the fray on Sunday. Miller played almost as well as Ballesteros tee to green but couldn't sink anything, and actually lost a stroke to par. The frustration was evident on his face.

I abandoned them on the ninth green and found Nicklaus on the practice tee, already through for the day, hitting practice wedges. He had finished his round with a 67, three under par, gaining some ground on the field but maybe not on the leaders. It was already apparent that Saturday's scores would be the lowest thus far.

Out on the golf course, Ballesteros gave back some shots on the back nine and finished up with a 68, tied for the tournament with Nicklaus and others at 216. Ben Crenshaw eagled the par-four fourteenth hole with his approach shot—then returned both strokes with a double bogey on fifteen. Crenshaw, though suffering, was still just four strokes behind Greg Norman, who maintained his lead on Saturday with a 71, but barely—one stroke over Hal Sutton, who shot a 66, and Lee Trevino, with a 69.

The big news of the day happened in my absence, but I've learned to expect that at a golf tournament. Norman had made the turn at nine with a four-stroke lead, but he bogeyed ten and double bogeyed the thirteenth hole with a drive into the right rough, an iron way over the green, a pitch back across the green, a chip, and a missed 4 footer (precisely how most of us would play the hole). After Norman's drive on the next hole, a grinning fan yelled that he was choking. The Australian heard him, turned, shook his club, and suggested he save his opinions until after the round. "If he'd said it to me anywhere else," Norman later told the press, "he'd have had a fistful of fingers."

That's a knuckle sandwich in the States, Greg, and such exchanges between pro and fan are rarely heard on golf courses. The proximity of New York City was my explanation. The crowds at the U. S. Open for tennis have never been the

same since that championship moved from the demure con-
fines of Forest Hills, Queens, to the public arena in Flushing
Meadows, across the street from Shea Stadium, home of the
Mets. Shinnecock Hills was an exclusive golf club, of course,
but the tournament crowd wasn't.

Norman quickly cooled off and salvaged the round with
five straight pars. I wasn't there. I had loaned my press pass to
Peter Chester, one of the Brooklyn foursome. He's a stalwart
Nicklaus fan who I knew would enjoy the post-round interview with the Golden Bear, and I didn't think anyone would
be terribly hurt by the unauthorized transfer of my pass for
thirty minutes. But I failed to take into account Chester's
attire for the day—big straw hat, Hawaiian shirt, white shorts,
sneakers, and, slung around his neck, a viewing periscope.
Where was his note pad? Chester wasn't going to fit in.

When I returned to the press tent at the agreed-upon
time—just about when Norman was having his problems with
the fan—Chester was sitting outside the door and didn't look
happy. My pass had been ripped off his Hawaiian shirt—
literally—by a USGA official. I should have known. Big-time
golf is a big deal, with a lot of big shots hanging around the
edges. So Chester was booted out of the press tent. However,
he got in a last laugh, of sorts. As he was sitting by the door
waiting for me, Nicklaus emerged—and autographed the
periscope.

Once Chester told me all about it, I got mad and walked
off the golf course and drove down to the beach. Boycott! My
idea right then was, To hell with this. I was tired and that was
my sixth straight day at Shinnecock Hills. Besides, almost
every time I write about golf I recall the twinge of embarrass-
ment I felt when I saw the movie *Shoot the Moon,* in which
the free-lance writer played by Albert Finney expresses to his
estranged wife (Diane Keaton) his jealousy of her earthy,
motherly accomplishments while all he was doing was "sitting

with my thumb up my ass, sharpening pencils and praying some editor would give me a pat on the back and some profile [to write] on the greenskeeper at Pebble Beach, and counting the goddamn dimples on the golf ball!"

That night we had a luau on the beach—me, my Sag Harbor hosts Ted (a Brooklyn golfer) and Betsy Wheeler, and Chester, the troublemaker. I tried a little surf casting until the reel fouled, then we hit shag balls on the deserted sand. After dinner we played boccie in a crude pit, and a young woman from Australia wandered up to our fire, just another stop on her tour of the world. Yes, she'd heard of Greg Norman, but a Norman victory in the U. S. Open the next day wouldn't mean much to her. I knew the feeling. She explained that she didn't have the energy to deal with current affairs because she was too busy trying to get her head together. In *America*, lady? You took a wrong turn somewhere. I was still mad.

11

⊙ ⊙ ⊙

A Calcutta is an illegal but widely acknowledged gambling enterprise in which the bettors bid on a player or team of players in a golf tournament. At the Ozona Invitational, the final eighteen holes on Sunday would conclude the thirty-six-hole championship, but they would also be played as a separate competition—the Calcutta. The Saturday night auction is officially termed a "team discussion," and everyone knows that's a joke.

Two years ago, the Calcutta at the Horseshoe Bay Tournament in Central Texas brought in $126,000. Four or five years ago, at the height of the oil boom, it had drawn almost $180,000. Jess Claiborne, one of the players from Lamesa competing in the Ozona Invitational, won the championship flight that year and was tipped well enough to buy a piece of land.

But in 1986, Horseshoe Bay had attracted only $11,500, a dispiriting sum that caused grave concern among the participants in Saturday night's auction at the Ozona Country Club. The previous high for a Calcutta in Ozona had been $40,000. If the decline in Ozona reflected the trend at Horseshoe Bay and other tournaments—and since the price of oil hadn't gone up, why wouldn't it?—the 1986 Invitational would be lucky to bring in $5,000, and that wouldn't be much fun or, for this journalist from New York City, very impressive.

But first we ate barbecue, the delicious slow-smoked briskets of Bill Glasscock. They were almost as good as the best barbecue in the world, the meat cooked by the now-deceased Casey Jones of Cut 'n' Shoot, Texas (yes, the home of boxer Roy Harris) and served out of a trailer house that couldn't handle the crowds.

The men folk in Ozona wore their golfing clothes to dinner, and the wives wore slacks or casual dresses. One young woman in a low-cut cocktail dress (such as I hadn't seen for years) was the main attraction. Then the food was cleared and the chairs turned toward one end of the big room, and everyone was provided with a Xeroxed list of all the teams and their scores for Saturday's round. The auctioneer's table was set up at one end of the room and I was invited to move up there to sit next to Mustard Williams, the auctioneer. Then club president Jim Adams, manager of the Wool Growers' Association, introduced me as the writer from up north on hand for the event, but he didn't mention my Ozona credentials, and that omission, I felt, left me twisting in the wind. A couple of people looked at me with puzzlement, and no wonder. How could I have even *found* Ozona without some local knowledge?

Williams appointed two spotters, one on each side of the room: Randy Poage, the highway engineer, and Winston Koerth, a first-flight golfer. The procedure was simple. A separate auction would be held for each flight, and the organizers of the tournament would take ten percent off the top for expenses (chiefly the evening's food and drink). The remaining sum would be split 50-30-20 for first-, second-, and third-place finishes in Sunday's round. If a gambler bought a lowly rated team for a cheap figure and his team took the top prize, his return would be many times his investment. The odds of finding such a dark horse weren't good, however. The golfers at the Ozona tournament knew each other and they knew how much credence to give to Saturday's scores.

The third-flight teams were the first up for bid, starting with the team with the worst score and moving up the list to the leaders. Twenty-five-dollar minimum, twenty-five-dollar increments. Mustard Williams explained the format, cued his spotters, took a sip of a pale liquid I understood to be hard liquor, and started the auction.

Nothing happened. The crowd of one hundred-plus sat on their hands. Nobody wanted the third-flight team of McMullan, McKinney, Mitchell, and Schneeman. After a quiet ten seconds, Pancho McMullan bid $25 on himself. Mustard Williams chided the audience, "Come on, these are the greatest hustlers in the county! Come on, now! I'm gonna sell 'em at that price. I tell ya, I'm gonna do it."

Silence.

"I am . . . *sold!*"

Dick Webster, sitting at the table and helping with the bookkeeping, glanced my way with raised eyebrows. A rock-bottom bid was a bad way to start off. The next team went for the $25 minimum to one of its members, and the next was bought cheap by a competitor, Pon Seahorn, my grandmother's banker.

Finally, the crowd managed some bidding for the top three teams in the flight. The rancher Pleas Childress had to pay $200 for his foursome, which was tied for the lead. Childress, it's safe to say, could have afforded to pay a good bit more, another zero or two or three, but he didn't look to me the type to go that high. But he didn't have to and was pleased with his bargain. Butch Gerber from Lamesa (formerly from Ozona) bought the leading team in that flight for $175.

The total pot for the third flight added up to a mere $825. Take ten percent off the top: The owner of the Calcutta winners on Sunday would earn less than $400, a grave disappointment.

Then the second flight netted only slightly more than the third flight, a sad $900. And without Butch Gerber's participation, it would have been less. The insurance man bought two teams for a total of $275, the equivalent strategy of betting on two horses in the same race. After that round of bidding Dick Webster looked over at me again. How bad could it be?

"Hell!" Mustard Williams yelled at one point, "They're gonna turn on the gas wells next week!"

Nobody believed him. The price of crude, as everybody knew, was frozen by the damn Arabs and the majors.

The most spirited bidding in a Calcutta is always reserved for the better golfers in the first and championship flights. For one thing, these flights would be less likely to produce some fluke winner from the ranks; the golfers were better known and they played better golf. But the first team in the first flight was sold for $25, the minimum again. Granted, their score for Saturday was sixteen strokes behind the leaders, so they probably weren't worth more than that. But the bidding stayed at that level for the next four teams. The big money, such as it was, wanted a piece of the top four teams in the flight, who were all within two strokes of the leaders. Mark Harvey, the contractor from Houston who had driven out early in the morning, bought his team for $225, after I dropped out of the bidding at $100. Butch Gerber bought the Dick and Rick Webster team for $175.

Grand total for the first-flight competitors: $1,075. The worst fears of the Ozona organizers had come true—there wasn't any loose money lying around Crockett County. More accurately, there was money, plenty of it, but not in the pockets of the newly rich big spenders from the oil patch who had jacked up the Calcutta pots all over the state three, four, five years ago. The ranchers, even the ones with the oil and gas underfoot, weren't going to bid that kind of money. They had nothing to prove.

"Twenty-five dollars! I can't believe this! This is the championship flight! Let's go!" Mustard Williams was beside himself as the last auction of the night began. He took a sip from his cup, leaned over to me, and whispered sotto voce, "You see? That's how bad it is in the oil patch!"

Whenever anyone mentioned this, I reminded him, good-naturedly of course, about the bumper sticker popular in Texas and other oil states just a few years ago, during the boom: LET THE DAMN YANKEES FREEZE IN THE DARK. With the tables now turned and plenty of cheap heating oil in the snow belt, even Texas Governor Mark White had conceded that he couldn't blame northerners for lacking sympathy for the plight of Texans. As much as I liked this Ozona bunch, I felt pretty much the same way. (White, a Democrat, was defeated two months after the Ozona Invitational by Bill Clements, an oil-patch Republican stalwart from Dallas.)

Not even the top four teams in the championship flight roused a great deal of interest. Butch Gerber bought his own Lamesa team for $150—a steal, I figured, and I regretted not topping him. The foursome from Fort Stockton went to their team leader, a banker named Harlan Lambert. Lambert sat at a table right in front of the auctioneer, wearing shorts and a straw hat, legs splayed, cigar protruding from his jaws, a man of action. I had hoped there would be dozens of this sort in Ozona, oil tycoons betting four figures as pocket change—Jett Rink types. (Rink was the James Dean character in *Giant*.) Lambert spent $200 on his foursome. Butch Gerber then hedged his bets and bought another team in his flight, the foursome with two top senior players I wanted to watch. The last team to be auctioned, a group of local aces just out of college, mostly, and led by rancher Rick Preston, went for the highest figure of the night, $375 from Preston. Total for the championship flight: $1,525.

The Calcutta was over. Grand total by my figures: $4,325. Under $5,000, indeed, while New York investment bankers and arbitrageurs and the Japanese were paying millions at Sotheby's for modern art not really suitable for anything but sale and resale, or donation and deduction. After the auction some of the golfers retired to the bar next door, but most went home or to the motel with their families. I sat on a table and talked with the Lamesa foursome of Gerber, Jess Claiborne, Art Ayres (who works for Claiborne's father in a chain of grocery stores) and Dennis Borland, a young player whose years of eligibility for college golf at nearby Angelo State had expired. This group had played in over fifteen four-man events around the western half of Texas that season.

Claiborne's teammates at Texas Christian University in the 1960s were mostly from West Texas, and he has a straight-forward theory to explain why that part of the state produces so many good golfers. "We can play on anything," he said, "because we've had to."

In 1979 Claiborne and a professional partner, Ronnie Rawson, played a match for $2,000 against a notorious hustler in West Texas, Billy Francis West, a black man, and his partner. The nine-hole match began about eight o'clock in the evening, and by the third hole the golfers were playing by the light of cars parked along the side of the fairways. The cars moved from hole to hole and Claiborne's team won the money. It was just another example of difficult conditions. "We play in sandstorms where you can't see the ball," Claiborne said matter-of-factly. "You have to feel where it went."

Gerber told me about another infamous Texas golfer, a man who rubs Chap Stick or some other grease on the face of his driver, to boost the ball off the clubhead. Later I mentioned this cheater to Dick Williams, who said, "Yes, I think he's the one who hasn't been invited back here."

Golf is a gentleman's game where everyone is on his honor because there's no one watching, for the most part, in amateur play. It necessarily follows that there are cheaters. Famous pros, including Gary Player, Bob Toski, and Jane Blalock, have been challenged, in widely publicized episodes, for fudging the rules. Much more common on the pro tours are incidents in which a pro calls a penalty on himself that no one would have known about otherwise (the ball moving slightly during address, usually). An amateur can usually get away with cheating. A classic way is to nudge a ball in the rough onto a better lie or to mark the ball on the green closer to the hole than it actually is. (The first golfer on the green can pick up his ball and toss his marker several feet in front of the right spot, all in one smooth motion.)

An objection raised to four-man events such as the Ozona Invitational is that each team of four plays alone. Nothing prevents a team from posting any reasonable score it desires. At two-man events, each foursome consists of two competing teams. They don't worry about it in Ozona. Honest golfers don't worry about cheaters because they presume that the cheating can help only marginally in most cases (much more than that in others, though, such as "finding" the lost ball, Oddjob's slick maneuver in *Goldfinger* when he dropped a new ball down his pants leg and then mutely pointed to it as the original. James Bond knew better because *he* had the original golf ball in his own pocket, but he won the match anyway.).

Butch Gerber asked me if I'd seen the story in the local paper about the exotic dancer. He was laughing about it, and indeed I had seen the piece and I was laughing, too. Under the headline EXOTIC DANCE PARTY ENDS IN SHOOTING, it read: "Ozona is not ready for exotic dancing. This was evident

Friday night when a party featuring this kind of entertainment was broken up by an irate wife with a loaded gun.

"A group had rented the old G. I. Forum Hall for an evening of festivities and entertainment. Just as activities were getting underway and the dancers giving forth with their most exotic routine, the wife of one of the party-givers entered and fired several shots from a .22 caliber pistol.

"One of the dancers was hit in the fleshy part of a thigh and hospitalized, and the party was effectively halted.

"Crockett County sheriff's personnel were on hand to quell any hostilities that might have arisen following the abrupt ending."

That was a stag party, of course, and Gerber remembers when MEN ONLY was the rule for almost all weekend activity in Ozona, and it wasn't all that long ago, either. The husbands went out to somebody's ranch for a weekend of hunting and fishing and drinking, and the wives stayed at home.

Sunday was another fairly cool day. A stiff wind blew from the northeast, a rare direction, and it made the par-three third hole/twelfth hole play very long. The first time around the course, the tee was set all the way back, and most of the field hit a wood, if not the driver. "Yeah," somebody said, "hit a driver into the hole and win a Suburban."

Someone else called out, within earshot of the banker Pon Seahorn, "I have about as much chance of winning that car as I do of getting a loan for one."

This was the hole on which a hole-in-one on the "back nine" would win the Chevy Suburban parked near the first tee. The tee on the par three was moved up for that back nine, but the shorter distance didn't help. Nobody won the vehicle. Eddie Hale, the high-handicapping goat roper, pulled his

drive on the hole way left, near an outhouse some forty yards
from the green. "Which hole wins that Suburban?" he called
out, to the general merriment of his group and the one
following. Another golfer hit a low screamer that landed short
of the green. He yelled, "Now run like you stole something."

In the championship flight Sunday afternoon was the
most unusual golf swing I've ever seen. Its owner was short
and skinny, and his practice swing looked fairly normal. But
when he addressed the ball, everything squinched up. His
body and his hands were much too close to the ball at address,
so as he moved into the ball on his downswing he had to jerk
up on his feet and jerk back with his arms and body. If he
hadn't done all this, he would have dug the clubhead into the
ground a foot behind the ball. This swing was hard to believe
in a championship-flight player, but the guy was playing
pretty well. He would have taken me to the cleaners on most
days, me and my (at one time) perfectly natural golf swing. He
must play all the time—there's no other way to produce any
consistency with a swing that bizarre—and he probably putts
like Ben Crenshaw.

I found the championship-flight team with the two renowned seniors, Jake Broyles and Roy Peden, both of whom
win tournaments all over the country. Broyles is rather tall
and moderately thin, and he picks the club straight up but
then makes a smooth shoulder turn—a two-piece backswing—and comes into the ball in good form. His partner
Peden is a heavy-set golfer of medium height who punches
the ball with all his weight. The two swings couldn't be more
different, nor the results more similar. Par golf, just about.

Butch Gerber is built about like Peden and hits the ball
in the same manner. Eight handicap. Jess Claiborne looks like
what he is, a former professional-caliber golfer with a classically smooth swing, although he was having trouble with
hooked drives for most of Sunday's round. One or two handi-

cap. Dennis Borland, the young player who had used up his college eligibility, was playing in red pants that weren't big enough, and I was surprised he didn't split the seams. He swung about as hard as I've seen anyone swing, almost as hard as the pro Mark Calcavecchia. Two or three handicap. Art Ayres, a tall man, and older than the others, had more of a seniors swing: long enough, always accurate. Six handicap.

In my role as roving reporter I was also used as roving scoreboard. Late in the day I told the Harlan Lambert foursome from Fort Stockton that they were leading or in a tie. "I don't want to put pressure on you," I added.

"Pressure?" Lambert exclaimed. "Pressure's all you know when you work in the oil patch!"

Maybe, but somehow his team faded on the final holes. Because of the shotgun start, the tournament finished on each of the nine holes at about the same time. A team wouldn't be sure how it had placed until it reported in at the scorer's desk on the patio, just outside the window in the wall through which the beer issued.

I found myself rooting for Butch Gerber's Lamesa team in the championship flight, but they came in third in the Calcutta, fourth overall. The young local aces took it all, the Calcutta by one stroke and the overall championship by three shots over Harlan Lambert's team. Add the Calcutta payoff of $686 to the $500 first prize, deduct the entry fee and the Calcutta bet, and Rick Preston's team netted over $600 for the weekend.

In the first flight a ringer team of Stuart, King, Clifton, and Hopkins won the Calcutta—a good payoff for a $75 bet. The team of Mike and David Williams, Duane Childress, and their contractor friend from Houston was second in both the Calcutta and the championship. Dick and Rick Webster's team was shut out.

In the second flight, the surprise was the Department of

Public Safety team: third place in the Calcutta, a profit of $62 for Butch Gerber, who had taken a flier on them Saturday night.

The team with Pon Seahorn and Epp Epperson, the rancher from Rocksprings who plays on sand greens, won the Calcutta in the third flight ($300 profit for Seahorn) and also third place in the championship. Horses Williams's team loped home second.

On Sunday evening, people had to get going. The Butch Gerber foursome drove their two golf carts onto the flatbed trailer and towed it up the highway toward Barnhart, on the way to Lamesa. The other carts were parked in the long sheds out back and hooked up to the battery chargers. The parking lot rapidly emptied of the sedans and station wagons, and I was one of the last to drive off, in my compact. I had with me some barbecue wrapped in tin foil and two gifts, an Ozona Country Club golf cap and towel, presented to me by B. W. Stuart, my grandfather's car dealer, the county commissioner who was voted out because of the softball fields—quite unfairly, I thought.

It was fun in Ozona, more fun than at Shinnecock Hills, in fact. Better food, better beer, more golf (based on the number of strokes per player), and I saw some golfers who were almost as good as the pros, *given the fact that they were amateurs*. The pros are pros; they should be better. I thought about the differences between the high-handicap players and the really good golfers in Ozona, and I answered the question I asked early in this book: Is it a silly notion or a great one, my idea that par golf or some facsimile (a low handicap) would confirm for me as well as anything might my capacity for commitment, achievement, and fulfillment? The answer must be: both.

It's silly because the game is a game and nothing more, no matter what the level of skill or competition, as Bobby

Jones declared on his early retirement from "the cage of championship." If Jones could walk away without damage to his psyche, surely I could have. If I really had quit the game after one of those infuriating rounds, so what?

But after his retirement, Jones expressed one chief regret. He had never proved that he could win an important championship without almost throwing it away first. And if I quit, I would always wonder why I hadn't been able just one time to play a mere eighteen holes for a dollar Nassau without losing my head. Why couldn't I play to my potential? It seems a great thing to at least keep trying.

12

⊙ ⊙ ⊙

I have two recurring dreams. In the first I'm a basketball player, and I float over and around all the defenders and dunk the ball with ease. When I take off I don't come down until I want to.

In the other I'm unable to hit my drive on the first tee. Things keep happening. The place and the details differ from night to night, but the gist of the story remains the same. First, perhaps, a large tree blocks my backswing. Then I'm too close to a wall behind me. Then the ball falls off the tee. Then I tee it up so far to the right that the ball washer's in the way. Then I realize I'm holding the wrong club in my hand, an eight-iron, not the driver. Then I notice I haven't put on my golf glove. And the ball is teed on a downslope and I have to move it. Then I need to switch clubs again. Then there are people standing in my way. This will go on for ten, fifteen, twenty contingencies, and I wake up every time without ever hitting that golf ball.

I could never dunk a basketball, but the dream made it easy. I can hit a good drive, but the dream makes that impossible. I don't understand this reasoning of my subconscious, but clearly it's frustrated with my inability to play the game consistently well. (I also realize both dreams might be explained in sexual terms, but who cares.)

I had that golf dream—or nightmare—for the first time in

quite a few years in Nairn, Scotland, and I know why. I was over there in July, during the British Open—before Ozona, after Shinnecock Hills. Throughout the summer I'd been working on my swing. A comeback by Bryan was the plan. After all, amateur golfers are always finding the secret and starting afresh, and I had learned important matters about my swing but hadn't worked much with that knowledge. Now I would assimilate that wisdom and start over, too, and report on the results. It'd be fun, I thought. Back to the roots of the game in Scotland—my game, *the* game. An excerpt from an anonymous English medieval ballad evokes the spirit of the adventure.

> *With an host of furious fancies,*
> *Whereof I am commander,*
> *With a burning spear and a horse of air,*
> *To the wilderness I wander.*
> *By a knight of ghosts and shadows*
> *I summoned am to tourney.*
> *Ten leagues beyond the wide world's end . . .*
> *Methinks it is no journey.*

I have boasted of my "perfectly natural golf swing," and I did make a sweet, smooth, and untutored pass at the ball. Then I realized I was undercutting that swing with too much hand action. About the same time, I figured out that I'd subtly instituted in my golf swing a tilting rather than a turning of the upper body. The tilt is an up-and-down movement in the vertical plane, mostly—right shoulder up, left shoulder down, while the spine and upper torso remain virtually still. A turn is more in the horizontal plane—right and left shoulders, and thus the torso, *around* the pivot of the spine. This is the turn that generates power in the golf swing. The tilt can feel like a turn because there's a lot of movement of the shoulders, but it's just worthless movement—quite literally, going through the motions. Maybe I'd always had a little tilt, even when people were commenting on my beautiful swing. At any rate, I had a terrible tilt when it was pointed out to me, and I didn't need a mirror to know the criticism was correct.

Too much hand action, tilting shoulders, not enough power generated by the swing: no wonder my game had broken down completely. I decided that for all those years all those golfers were complimenting my swing, it was probably faulty, the tilt well concealed by a fluid motion, the excess manipulation of the hands at impact undetected. Sometime during that period of enlightenment I was talking with Steve Melnyk, a former pro and now a television announcer, and he mentioned that his swing had degenerated to such a point that he was having to address the ball far back in his stance. "I was trapping the ball," he said. "That was the only way I could be sure of hitting it at all with my upright stance." My eyebrows shot up. I'd been addressing the ball way back in my stance, too! Melnyk explained that putting the ball back there makes it easier to hit with an upright stance. It all made sense.

My wife was tired of seeing me hassle with the game, and during the frustrating overhaul of my swing she arranged for me to take a lesson from Hank Haney, a renowned teaching pro in Houston who has since moved his operation to California. I was furious at her audacity and said I wasn't going—I was playing very little golf at the time—but then I went and was glad I did. I hit a few balls for Haney and was about to launch into my complex analysis when he preempted me, pointing out everything I was about to say and much more. Then he told me what to do about it. After a couple of hours on his practice range at the Sweetwater Country Club, I was hitting good draws with the 5-iron off a tee. I had a good shoulder turn, a flatter swing plane, and I used my body more and my hands less. I picked up the basics of that swing quickly (or, conceivably, I recalled them after many, many years), but it felt new to the point of seeming foreign. I knew I could never transport this practice-tee success to the golf course without a great deal of work. Haney said so, too, and he urged me not to even try to hit a wood like that for a while, and to hit only teed-up irons until I was thoroughly comfortable with the feeling of the new form.

I didn't practice. I just played some, modifying the new swing for shots off the turf, but adhering to it strictly with my tee balls. I hit the driver, too, and often very well. At an outing at Quaker Ridge Golf Club in Westchester County to benefit Holy Cross College (my friend the former Brooklyn golfer Gene Keogh was the organizer who hit me up for the donation), I struck more good drives than I ever had in a single round, and decent irons. I was playing golf. I knew I was hitting the ball correctly. I could feel the body working, the hands more passive. I developed a few keys to carefully establish in my head before I swung, and if I did so, I hit the ball well. If I didn't, I threw it out to the right, but that didn't bother me. It was a failure in my mind, I reasoned, not in my swing. For the first time in more years than I could remember, I knew I had the correct swing at my disposal. I just knew it. I could gear up my mind when I had to, I told myself. When I really cared about playing the game again, I'd concentrate, establish those swing keys, and hit the ball fine. I would start doing that for keeps in Scotland.

I was prepared to love Scottish golf courses because they're wide open to the wind and the sky. Lots of vista. I wasn't disappointed by the first course I saw, Prestwick St. Nicholas, which was right across the railroad tracks from the house my wife and I were staying at in Prestwick, on the Ayrshire coastline. On the other side of the golf course was the beach. Of course I'd seen many TV broadcasts from many Scottish courses, so I knew basically what to expect. Nevertheless, to walk out on that golf course, an honest-to-goodness links, was frankly thrilling. How plain and ordinary and un-prepossessing it was: some vaguely manicured swaths for fairways, greens flat on the contour of the land, likewise the bunkers, and unkempt rough—all of it utterly unremarkable terrain. If Augusta National is the jewel box and Shinnecock Hills an earthier piece of work, a jewel in the rough, then Prestwick St. Nicholas is raw coal. I loved it.

It was cold on the golf course, with showers rushing past every few minutes and lasting about that long, and wind howling off the water. A man playing alone—there weren't a dozen players out altogether—walked past and said, "A bit blowy."

Not very treey, either. That golfer and his landscape direct me to this observation of Arnold Haultain's in *The Mystery of Golf,* an early classic about the game: "You can detect national character in games. Golf is preeminently the game of the Scot: slow, sure, quiet, deliberate, canny even—each man playing for himself. Compare it with cricket, the game of the typical Anglo-Saxon of more southern proclivities. . . . In cricket you have an ally or allies, both in batting and in fielding; it is communistic, political. The nation that evolved cricket evolved the British Constitution."

Prestwick St. Nicholas had been used the previous week for qualifying rounds for the British Open, just getting under-way that Thursday at Turnberry, thirty miles to the south. A mile to the north is Old Prestwick, a rugged warhorse that had been used for the Open until logistical factors ruled it out.

Tom Watson's wife once said that all you need in order to have fun at the British Open is long underwear. But despite our layered T-shirts, long-sleeved shirts, sweaters, and windbreakers, my wife and I were freezing at Turnberry on Friday—and Friday was less blowy and perhaps a little less cold than Thursday, which everyone agreed was one of the worst days in modern British Open history. The scores made those in the first round at Shinnecock Hills look excellent. Saturday was marginally warmer but even windier. One big difference between the American and the British Opens, I noticed immediately, was the galleries. They're dour in Scotland—no obligatory applause after the golfer holes out—or maybe they're just sitting on their hands to keep them warm. On the other hand, they're alike in this respect: In Scotland, too, Jack Nicklaus had by far the biggest galleries. Despite Tom Watson's five British Open victories and his unabashed love for Scotland, despite the presence in the field of a Scotsman as defending champion—Sandy Lyle, now living in England— and despite all the other top British and Irish players, Nicklaus remained the crowd's favorite.

The Ailsa course at Turnberry (there is another eighteen, the Arran) is more dramatic than Prestwick St. Nicholas, with greater changes of elevation, a more stunning coastline to overlook, and more obviously handcrafted greens and bunkers. Only the rough at Turnberry is left untended. The golf course was requisitioned as a staging area during the Second World War and three fairways were paved over for landing strips. Substantially rebuilt after the war, it's now a polished if rugged course in all respects, in the Shinnecock Hills mode, the intermediate stage between the piece of coal and the polished gem, watched over by the magnificent hotel that faces it and the sea.

Turnberry will always be remembered as the site of the unprecedented shootout between Watson and Nicklaus for the 1975 Open championship, when Watson fired 65-65 the final two rounds to beat Nicklaus's 65-66 by that single stroke. The two men were paired with each other both days, and standing on the fourteenth tee during the last round Watson said to Nicklaus, "This is what it's all about, isn't it?" And Nicklaus responded, "It sure is." Played at that level of skill, I suppose so. This may be the biggest difference of all between their game and mine, between them and me: the passion to win. I've never felt that way about any competition. I play hard, I'd rather win, but whether I do is unimportant. The playing is the thing for me. One reason I've never converted my nice swing (too much hand action and some recent tilting notwithstanding) into steady golf might be that I haven't really cared enough. The desire to beat someone certainly helps develop excellence, but I've always played golf for those "aesthetic" reasons cited earlier: the cool feel of the game.

One enjoyment on the golf course I do share with Watson and Nicklaus is the pleasure of playing with friends. Most of the pros have fairly steady practice partners; this, for them, is recreational golf. Most amateurs have steady foursomes. I didn't appreciate the importance of this until I read *Golf in the Kingdom*. The American visitor Michael and the Scottish pro Shivas Irons and some other golfers are analyzing the mysterious siren call of the game, but it's the wife of one of the men who gets to the heart of the matter—or so it seemed to me. After listening to theories about the yoga of the supermind, the next manifesting plane, and a physics of the spirit—mental-side stuff raised to the highest power—Agatha McNaughton says they're all beside the point. Golf, she argues, is about men loving men.

"It's the only reason ye play at all. It's a way ye've found to get together and yet maintain a proper distance. I know you men. . . . All those gentlemanly rools, why, they're the proper tools of affection—all the waitin' and oohin' and ahin' o'er yer shots, all the talk o' this one's drive and that one's putt and the other one's gorgeous swing—what is it all but love? Men lovin' men, that's what golf is."

And then: "Oh, golf is for smellin' heather and cut grass and walkin' fast across the countryside feelin' the wind and watchin' the sun go down and seein' yer friends hit good shots and hittin' some yerself. It's love and it's feelin' the splendor o' this good world."

I believe she's right—and I suppose this discussion could substitute women for men and be just as accurate, but I'm in no position to know. Something else had happened about the time I was shanking those shots at the Westchester Country Club, and preparing (without knowing it) to leave the job with the magazine, and the game. The Brooklyn foursome was breaking up. Gaskins moved to Minneapolis. Chester moved to Connecticut. Keogh stayed in Brooklyn but joined a club in Westchester. I would have said that I was never one to pal around with the guys—male bonding and all that—but in fact that's just what those golf games in New Jersey were all about, right down to the beer in the bar in the clubhouse afterwards, parsing the scorecard for half an hour to determine the winners of myriad two-bit bets.

I'll state this bluntly. The game is more fun played with a regular group of guys. I believe this holds true for the increasing number of men who used to play the game with a regular foursome but who now, in retirement, play mostly with their wives. However, I'm not going to ask my father to go on record in this regard. What Bobby Jones wrote about inexorable fate and tangled personalities is absolutely correct, but it's not the whole reason we play the game. The treklike nature of golf in companionship with other players is an important element in its appeal. In a way, golf is just a group of men on a hunt.

Greg Norman shot a 63 on a windy Friday at Turnberry to blow into a two-shot lead over Gordon Brand. On Saturday Norman slipped to a 74 but was still leading. On Sunday—I wasn't there. I hadn't gone to Scotland to see the Open, anyway, and my wife and I were disgruntled with the solid cloud cover over the western coastline, so early Sunday morning we headed north toward Nairn. Our strategy backfired. We were in clouds all day, while the radio reported that the sun had broken through back at the championship, for a lovely final round.

We arrived on the north coast Monday morning and I called ahead to Nairn to see whether I could play that afternoon—visiting American golf writer, in the country for the Open, and so on.

Of course, come on by. Almost all of the Scottish courses are playable by touring golfers, even with short notice or none at all. The Nairn links were just about empty when we drove up and I was set up for an immediate tee-off with Bill Brown, a member, and his son Andrew. I had about three minutes to get my shoes on and my head together, a hurried beginning to my new career in golf.

We were playing into the teeth of a gale. Tuck the right elbow, turn the shoulders, swing slowly. Those were my swing keys but they broke down sometime between when I put the ball on the tee with shaking fingers and when I started my backswing. I was way too quick and the ball ducked off to the left into some grass about a foot high. Bill Brown hit a straight shot and so did Andrew. Later I missed a 1 footer on the green that surprised me with its slickness.

On two I topped my drive, pull-hooked the 3-wood, chili-dipped the 3-iron, then hit a straight 5-iron but took a bunch of putts on the green. Bill Brown was losing heart by now, and I wasn't feeling much better myself. This was no way to start a new life. On three I finally hit the driver solidly, but a little right onto the beach. I dropped off the beach, pull-hooked my 3-wood, took three or four shots to get out of a deep, deep bunker (one of three hundred on the links), only to land in another bunker. I picked up.

Bill Brown and Andrew excused themselves. They suddenly had to go home for dinner. I didn't blame them. My patient wife wasn't saying a word, and I didn't blame her either. She has seen me get mad on a golf course. I hadn't speared one at Nairn yet, but she considered it possible and she was right. On the fourth hole I hit a perfect drive into the gale: a couple of hundred yards, dead straight. On the next hole we met John Bochel, a local member who was playing alone, and joined him for the rest of the round. Amazingly, I hit a lot of straight shots. The keys were under control, for the most part, but when they collapsed the result was disastrous. Over those first holes, quite simply, I had panicked.

Nairn is much closer to Prestwick St. Nicholas than it is to Turnberry—just a golf course out there on the links—and a very hard course if you don't hit the ball straight. The virulent unmowed rough is the problem all visiting Americans have with links layouts; every fairway might as well be bordered by water. After those awful first holes I had given up keeping score, in conscious defiance of the admonition of Shivas Irons in *Golf in the Kingdom,* who warned Michael, the book's "ugly American," of the dangers of taking scorekeeping lightly. It's a measure of the man, he said, more than of the golf. Keep score and keep it right. But I didn't want to be measured that day, and that, naturally, is exactly Shivas's point. We have no choice but to be measured every day.

John Bochel was a pleasant playing partner—we were about even in ability—and he also set my wife and me up with a good place to spend the night. He and I had such an enjoyable round that we arranged to meet Tuesday morning for an early game before my wife and I left for Edinburgh, St. Andrews, and Muirfield.

That night in Nairn I had the dream—the nightmare. Toward the end of it, the green for the first hole was on top of the tall tower on the University of Texas campus. I didn't know what kind of shot to hit, and I woke up. Poltergeist was back . . . again. But I played pretty well with John Bochel on Tuesday, without keeping score. It seemed pointless. I felt good about my swing, but knew I couldn't score decently on these golf courses with hayfields for rough. In two brief days I had gone from "starting over with a clean slate" to "working on my swing, for god's sake, what do you expect!"

St. Andrews is a lovely little place, with the golf course wedged between the town and the North Sea. I don't suppose there's another course in the world situated like St. Andrews, with the town literally right across the street, hugging the flanks of the golf course on two sides. Ben Crenshaw has many times expressed the wish that every golfer could play a round at St. Andrews, where golf is played just about as it has been for hundreds of years. Only the equipment has changed. The town owns the layout, which isn't much to look at but is a subtle test of golf, and families cross it on their way to the adjacent public beach. Dogs run free. Clergymen and shopkeepers play side by side, a Sunday bag slung over the shoulder, and a round takes three hours or less.

That's how I imagined St. Andrews, at any rate, but I ended up in a foursome with a southern Californian, an Australian, and a Japanese—Jim, Steve, and Mira. Judging by the crowds of obvious tourists standing around with or without tee times, I wondered when the locals played. I sprang for an AA caddie, which means a caddie old enough to fit every golfer's image of a dour Scotsman, licensed to say anything he wants about your game. After I pulled my drive on the third hole, old Ralph Morris said calmly, "Good thing the fairways are wide for you."

"I'll straighten out," I assured him.

"Good."

I was scraping the ball around for bogeys, mainly, with nervous swings—St. Andrews, after all!—and then on the sixth hole it happened. Ralph gave me the line for the drive, I hit a nice long draw on the short hole, starting the ball way out over the rough, bringing it back. I knew I could do it because I was hitting the ball better with every hole. I only had a little wedge left to the green. The wedge. I thought of the debacle at Westchester Country Club. I thought of Johnny Miller. What was called for at St. Andrews was the wedge preventative. There is a way not to shank a golf shot, at least for me not to, and that's to take over with the hands at the last moment and, in all likelihood, send the ball left. A pull, but not a shank. Cowardly, but not deflating. I came in with my hands, all right, but too much so, and served up a chili dip.

You just can't play golf worrying about the damn wedge shot. That's a game not worth playing. On the next attempt I said to hell with it, just hit the ball.

"Soul destroying," Ralph said quietly, and gracefully dropped another ball after the shank disappeared into the brush.

On the eleventh hole, Bobby Jones took four shots to get out of the bunker that now bears his name. I was in there, too, but I was playing the seventh hole, which shares a gigantic green with eleven (there are six other double greens on the Old Course, its most famous features). I bogeyed my way around most of the back nine, hitting some nice shots and avoiding the wedge. To score decently at St. Andrews isn't hard if you avoid the bunkers and the rough. Nevertheless, it features a kind of golf many American pros can't tolerate: blind shots, hidden bunkers, terrible bounces, inevitable wind. These pros want big, fat greens soft enough to accept any line drive, fairways as wide as a football field, sand traps shallow and easy to play out of (whereas some in Scotland are equipped with ladders, and you need them). They want new American courses that succumb to one kind of golf and one only: raw power.

On seventeen, the famous Road Hole that bends around a hotel before concluding at the green with a road directly behind it and in play, three of our foursome nailed drives onto the roof of the building, trying to cut the dogleg too much.

"You make it hard on yourselves," Ralph offered.

On eighteen, which returns to the clubhouse adjacent to the first hole and shares a fairway that must be one hundred yards wide, I was just over the green with my iron, the ball almost against the low fence on which tourists were lounging. I imagined Jack Nicklaus surging through the gallery here in 1978, when he won his last of three British Open titles. But I couldn't imagine it.

In 1984 Nicklaus was the first sportsman awarded an honorary degree by the University of St. Andrews, founded in 1410, the oldest in Scotland. In his acceptance remarks he said that the walk along that flat fairway was the most memorable experience of his life. Perhaps now the walk up the hill on eighteen at The Masters in 1986 is on a par with it.

In 1958 Bobby Jones was honored by the town of St. Andrews with the "Freedom of the City." He had won the Open at St. Andrews in 1927 and the Amateur in 1930, and in subsequent visits won the hearts of the local citizenry. One other American has been so honored—Benjamin Franklin, in 1759. Accepting the award in a ceremony in Younger Hall at the University of St. Andrews, Jones said, "I could take out of

my life everything except my experiences at St. Andrews and
I'd still have a rich, full life."

My chip was short, and I took two putts for the final
bogey. I didn't break 100, not with a couple of snowmen or
worse. Just working on my swing, you know. After the round I
poked my head into the austere St. Andrews clubhouse, home
of the ruling body in Britain. Gents were walking around in
jackets. Benches outside were marked MEMBERS ONLY. Yet
the golf course right outside the front door is open to one and
all.

The following day, Muirfield, universally acknowledged
as one of the great layouts in the world, and *the* greatest layout
was the vote at *Golf Magazine* when I was in charge of
publishing the poll. That accolade is what got me onto the
course. Unlike most Scottish links, Muirfield requires you to
write months in advance, establish some pedigree, beg forbearance—and you *might* be invited to play. This was never
more difficult than in the days of the infamous Captain Paddy
Hanmer, who enjoyed escorting hopeful American golfers
onto the course, looking around at the almost empty links,
and remarking, "Quite full, really." That, anyway, is the joke
about Hanmer.

Now everything is well organized and official at Muirfield, and on Tuesdays, Thursdays, and Friday mornings the
golf course is turned over to golfers visiting from all the world
over. Along with my letter of acceptance I received "Notes for
the guidance of visitors playing at Muirfield." Strangest point:
They don't have a pro shop, which is unheard of elsewhere in
the free world. In addition to strange wardrobes, golfers have
an obsessive desire for towels and other mementos inscribed
with the names of famous courses they've played.

Relatively new by Scottish standards, Muirfield opened
in 1925, replacing an older course built in 1891, the year the
Shinnecock Hills Golf Club and the town of Ozona were
founded. That early course had replaced layouts in nearby
Leith and Musselburgh as the official home of the Honourable
Company of Edinburgh Golfers—the official name of the
club. The modern Muirfield is a set of fairways through a field,
each green beautifully bunkered, each hole a classically
straightforward test of golf. While St. Andrews features a
thousand hidden hazards, at Muirfield what you see is what
you get, and all pros love this lack of tomfoolery.

My wife and I were late driving up and I raced to park
the car, get the spikes on, and hit the first drive in the
company of my caddie, Tom Hutchison, a local retired maintenance engineer. A fellow from Canada and his wife were
waiting for me down the fairway. For all my lousy golf over the
years, I usually hit a good drive on the first hole. I must
concentrate better, knowing that everyone standing around is
watching—it's difficult not to watch a golfer hit on the first tee.
But so far in Scotland, I'd choked every time—and at Muirfield I topped the ball, something I hardly ever do. It must
have been an awful swing. Tom Hutchison suggested quietly
that I take a mulligan and slow down. I jerked the next ball
left into the hay.

I never got going in that round of golf. I hit a number of
good drives, but usually followed up with weird irons, always
with that shank in the back of my mind. When I rolled in a 30-
footer on eighteen for something way over 100, I was happy to
be through. My wife and I left quickly. The clubhouse and the
locker room are museums, old pictures and history everywhere, but I've never been interested in that stuff. Besides,
they don't allow women in the dining room.

13

I didn't go into the press room at Shinnecock Hills on Sunday. They could have my press pass.

Seventeen pros had broken par on Saturday, one quarter of the field of seventy. That was about right, I thought. That many professionals should break par on a course set up fairly. Shinnecock Hills was a success as a golf course and as a tournament. Fourteen players started the final round within four shots of the leader, easy striking range, and seven others were within six strokes, not an impossible deficit. Twenty-one players with a conceivable chance to win on the last day: That's a great national championship.

At one point on the front nine, seven players were tied for the lead at +1: Greg Norman, the leader by one at the start of play, Lee Trevino, Payne Stewart, Ben Crenshaw, Hal Sutton, Bob Tway, and Mark McCumber. Just after these leaders made the turn onto the back nine, Lanny Wadkins, the free swinger who had started six strokes behind Norman, finished his round with a 65, tying for the course record (which Mark Calcavecchia set earlier in the day) and posting a total of +1. That's almost the only way to shoot such a low number on the final round of the Open—start ahead of the leaders, play under less pressure, finish early. When I watched on tiptoe from behind a big crowd as Wadkins made the 4 footer for par on eighteen, I thought he was the winner.

I think *he* believed he might be the winner after his birdie on the long par-five sixteenth; he literally strutted off that green. Wadkins is a cocky guy, and that's necessary in order to play the game as he plays it, all out on every shot.

When Wadkins posted his +1 total he was one behind Stewart and Sutton on the scoreboard, but I didn't have much faith in either of those two golfers' prospects of playing the last nine holes at Shinnecock Hills at level par to win the Open. Indeed, neither one did. The rule in the Open is that the leaders come back to the rest of the field on the back nine, recording a lot more bogeys than birdies, and this was true of all but one of the leaders at Shinnecock Hills.

Following Wadkins into the clubhouse with a +1 total was Chip Beck, a solid young player who also shot a 65 after starting the day six shots back. Beck sank birdie putts on the tenth, eleventh, twelfth, thirteenth, and fifteenth greens. (No contradiction here to the premise that the leaders back up, since Beck wasn't a leader when he started his run.) Both Beck's and Wadkins's rounds of 65 proved once again that the key in golf is to keep grinding, keep playing. Average golf for sixty-three holes can be compensated for by nine terrific holes, as Jack Nicklaus had just proved at The Masters.

I wanted Ben Crenshaw to win, but he let his chances slip away when he missed makable birdie putts, of about fifteen and twenty feet on ten and eleven, and then bogeyed twelve. The twelfth tee is elevated, and the wind from the south and the southwest on Sunday cut across the fairway from left to right, and slightly behind the player. After his drive Crenshaw exclaimed, "Damn! Wind!" That, I thought, was about as angry as he was going to get, but on the next hole he was short of the green with his iron and threw down his cap. I had to smile. The gesture indicated anger, but his expression didn't. Then he missed from eighteen inches for a bogey, and that was it for my sentimental favorite.

Sutton was making *Golf Digest* look good. The editors had picked him as its 11-to-1 second choice at Shinnecock Hills ("Back on top after '84 slump"), right behind their favorite, Calvin Peete, at 10-to-1 ("Open setup tailor-made for 'Mr. Accuracy'"). However, actually betting on the winner of a golf tournament is foolish. Judging conservatively, twenty to thirty players had a chance to win, and few had particularly better chances than any of the others. As judged by the standards of horse racing or tennis, all were long shots. For any golfer in the field, the odds of missing the cut after Friday's round were better than the odds of winning the tournament.

Sutton is the only major player of recent years to have given even a passing thought to remaining an amateur golfer. The son of a wealthy Louisiana oilman, he could have worked in the business and played gentleman's golf had he put aside his ambition to be the best. In Bobby Jones's era, sixty years ago, a great player could remain an amateur and compete with the pros, and beat them. The professional game hadn't reached the caliber of the competition today, nor was there any financial incentive to turn pro. In those days, the leading money winners made less than ten thousand dollars. Today the amateur golfer doesn't have a prayer against the pros, with Scott Verplank's victory as an amateur the exception that proves the rule. If Sutton wanted to see how good he was, he'd have to turn pro. And once he did, he was hailed as the heir apparent to Nicklaus. THE BEAR APPARENT read the headlines. (I admire the subtle irony of this statement by Bobby Jones in *Golf Is My Game:* "Many times I have been asked why I retired from competition in golf, but no one has ever asked me how I got into the thing in the first place. Perhaps this is just as well, for there were reasons for quitting and none for starting. The beginning just began, as it often does.")

Hal Sutton won the last tournament of his first season,

1982, and twice in 1983—the PGA Championship, a major, and the Tournament Players Championship. He was the leading money winner on the tour in his sophomore year. He played well but was winless in 1984, so when he won twice in 1985 the stories were different. He was no longer considered the inevitable great star of the future. No one is today—with the possible exception of Greg Norman.

Alas, Norman never got going on Sunday. Accompanied all day by two cops intended to discourage the hecklers of Saturday (they did), Norman struggled and admitted after the round that he just felt flat, especially after missing from four feet for par on the sixth hole. But he birdied the next one. The flatness came to the fore between the ninth and thirteenth holes, with four bogeys in five holes. Did Norman choke? Before the tournament even started, some fans and golf writers were wondering about his ability to win majors. After all, he had sprayed a 6-iron into the bleachers on the last hole of the Open at Winged Foot in 1984 and had to sink a monstrous par-putt to save a tie with Fuzzy Zoeller; then, in the eighteen-hole playoff, Zoeller took him to the cleaners. On the last hole at The Masters, two months before Shinnecock Hills, when a shot to the middle of the green and two putts for par would have tied him with Nicklaus, Norman missed right and took a bogey.

After the '84 Open, Norman acknowledged the bad iron shot but pointed to the long putt he subsequently sank as the critical shot. After The Masters, he explained he'd tried to "do too much" with the 4-iron that strayed to the right. He didn't point out that he followed the poorly struck iron with a fine, delicate chip and a beautiful putt that could just as easily have rolled in (just as Tom Kite's could have rolled in). And he didn't mention his four consecutive birdies on the fourteenth through the seventeenth holes. If the iron was a choke, what about all the clutch birdies?

The pros do choke, of course, if that's defined simply as making a bad shot under pressure. The muscles know the swing and are ready to produce it, but the mind's knowledge of the situation—in a word, tension—leaks out into the real world of muscles, ligaments, joints, and alignments. On the other hand, what's the proof that the critical moment caused the bad shot? After all, pros make bad shots at other times, too. And after producing lousy shots at the worst possible time, they'll turn around and make an incredible recovery. Did the center fall apart, and then get put back together again?

Some players deny the whole idea of choking, while others cheerfully admit to it. The notoriously carefree Fuzzy Zoeller even boasts that he doesn't mind gagging. He enjoys the pressure moments, he says, and sometimes he'll make the shot and sometimes he won't—and if you want to call the mistake a choke, that's fine by him. In baseball parlance: You win some, you lose some, and some are rained out. That's the basic attitude of most professional athletes, and perhaps hidden between the lines is a quiet disdain for the fans who have no idea what's really going on out there, and for the writers who mainly are looking for a juicy story.

Johnny Miller is loose enough to joke about choking—grabbing his throat in a gagging gesture—even when tense enough to produce the bad shot in the first place. (You can't, however, imagine Jack Nicklaus horsing around like this.) Andy Bean might grab his throat, too. Thirty-three years old in 1986, at the peak of his career, Bean has won about one golf tournament a year for a decade. He is one of the dozen best players on the tour—but he is never won a major, and has finished second only twice. Therefore, when he's occasionally asked about this failing by an intrepid reporter, the implied question is, "Are you a choker?"

Bean doesn't punch the guy out. Instead, he looks directly at his accuser, says something like "It hasn't happened yet, but it will," and then dismisses him forever from his universe. Indeed, the record doesn't establish Bean as a choker. If it did, Sam Snead was a life-long choker in the U. S. Open—no victories, and four second-place finishes including a playoff loss by one shot.

Bobby Jones had these thoughts on choking—a term he didn't use—in *Golf Is My Game:*

> Whatever lack others may have seen in me, the one I felt most was the absolute inability to continue smoothly and with authority to wrap up a championship after I had won command of it. The failing cost me the eventual winning of more than one, and made several others look a lot more fortuitous than they should have. . . .
>
> As nearly as I can analyze my own state of mind, up to the point of becoming aware that I was the winner I had been possessed of a singleness of purpose driven by an intense desire to win, which had of itself focused my concentration upon playing golf. . . .
>
> Having reached a stage where I suddenly knew that I should certainly win with any sort of ordinary finish, I became fearful of making myself look ridiculous by kicking the thing away. At this point, I think I began to be conscious of my swing and began trying to make too certain of avoiding a disastrous mistake. I was no longer playing the shots for definitive objectives, but was rather trying to keep away from hazardous places.

So Bobby Jones choked, too. But he also wrote:

> In at least two matches, those with Tolley and Voigt at St. Andrews, I had been outplayed throughout; and in the final round of each of the Open championships I had

made mistakes of grievous proportions. On several occasions I had lost control of my game. But having once found myself in these dire predicaments, I had managed, from the point of realization, to drive myself to the end, when it would have been easy, even pleasant, to play the "give-up" shot.

And this final thought from Jones, from *Down the Fairway:*

I think a man may be a truly great golfer and not be a great tournament golfer; and I do not think that the customary implication, that a great golfer who fails to shine at formal competition lacks courage, is justified. Matters of physique and mere physical stamina have a profound effect, as do also personal inclination and taste. Then there is that curious and little understood factor of temperament, which is so convenient an explanation either of the successful tournamenteer or the unsuccessful one.

In any event, I maintain that golf and tournament golf are two different things. . . . I had a remarkably good opportunity to study the difference.

On Sunday at Shinnecock Hills, Greg Norman either choked or simply had a bad round. Your choice. On Sunday at Turnberry, in the final round of the British Open, he played solid golf and won going away.

I picked up the twosome of Ray Floyd and Payne Stewart on the fourteenth hole. Stewart had birdied twelve to take the lead, but then bogeyed thirteen while Floyd hit an iron stiff for the birdie. They were then tied with Sutton for the lead at even par. Of those three, the betting man would have rushed to the window right then to put his money down on Floyd, known among the players as one of the hardest competitors on the tour. He had thrown away the Westchester tournament the week before the Open with a 77 in the final round—an inexplicable finish, since Floyd is considered a solid front-runner. Floyd and his wife, Maria—whom he pretty much credits with settling him down and saving his pro career in the late sixties—had discussed that debacle, seeking ways to learn from it. When Lanny Wadkins turned in his one-over-par total, I didn't know Floyd was easing into the picture. Now that he was tied for the lead with five holes to play, I didn't believe it was likely that he'd fade for the second week in a row. Why Floyd hadn't really challenged in any of his previous twenty-two U. S. Opens is a mystery. He had finished in the top ten only twice. He's exactly the kind of smart player who figured to do well in the Open, but he hadn't.

Both he and Stewart flew their approach shots to the middle of the green on fourteen, and both balls bounced over. Stewart chipped long and missed his par coming back. Floyd chipped to four feet and sank the putt. Since Sutton had bogeyed in the meantime, Floyd was all alone in the lead. And that's when the house shut the betting window.

On fifteen, Stewart salvaged par with an 8 footer and Floyd, after missing from six feet for birdie, didn't even flinch. He hadn't grinned after the birdie on thirteen, either. He was totally in the game. After the tournament, his wife said that she saw "that look" in his eyes on the back nine and quit worrying. It's true, Floyd's bluish eyes freeze up into hard little marbles (if not "the look of eagles," good enough).

Back on the twelfth hole, playing several groups behind Floyd and Stewart, was Hal Sutton. His drive rolled under a scrubby bush, from where he chunked the ball across the fairway—all he could do—and bogeyed another hole. He never charged after that. Bob Tway ran out of time, too, and even shanked his second shot on the sixteenth hole. Lee Trevino couldn't make birdies. Mark McCumber made a couple of bogeys.

Floyd won the tournament on sixteen after he backed away from his third shot on the par five to reprimand a photographer—"Don't take snapshots till I hit, please!"—then turned back to the shot and knocked his 8-iron ten feet from the pin. All week long on the practice tee I had watched players making punch shots with a low trajectory, but over the weekend most of those I saw on that sixteenth hole were hitting their regulation high lobs into the wind, pure guesswork. Floyd, a shotmaker of the old school, rammed his ball beneath the breeze on Sunday, then he sank the putt.

The concern of the galleries and TV viewers would usually have been, Can Floyd hang on? The defensive posture of leaders in the Open is usually quite evident, but I don't believe anyone on the course had those doubts about Floyd. He surely didn't have them about himself: Every shot the last two holes was right on the nose, never in doubt. In April, Nicklaus became the oldest player to win The Masters, at age forty-six; in June, at age forty-three, Floyd became the oldest to win the Open. And just as Nicklaus had been overlooked prior to The Masters, so was Floyd unlisted by the odds makers of *Golf Digest*.

On tape I saw his remarks following the round, when he was close to tears. "Realistically," he said, "I felt today I had to do it. It was probably my last chance."

During the television broadcast, Frank Hannigan, Executive Director of the USGA and one of the men responsible for bringing the tournament to Shinnecock Hills, reminded viewers that Ray Floyd had been Ken Venturi's playing partner in the 1964 Open at Congressional, when Venturi staggered home a winner in the heat. Floyd dipped into the cup on eighteen to retrieve Venturi's final putt, and there were tears in his eyes as he handed the ball to the new champion.

Dave Eichelberger's 66 on Sunday clinched best-comeback honors, at least for that one tournament. After opening with an 80, his revamped swing produced three fine rounds of 70-72-67. Mac O'Grady went the other way, finishing over the weekend with a disappointing 73-77, and I wondered whether he hadn't become distracted from the golf by his good position at the halfway mark and his lengthy interview in the press tent Friday evening. Three weeks later he won the Sammy Davis tournament in Hartford. Jack Nicklaus's closing 68 left him just five strokes behind Floyd, and in a televised interview after his round the announcers asked whether he rued his six-over-par back nine on Thursday. Nicklaus would have none of it, and pointed out that Floyd had some trouble on Thursday, too—everyone had. Nicklaus, Floyd, all the great players have won some titles they perhaps shouldn't have, and lost some they should have won, nor would they have it any other way; nor would Bob Eaks, Thomas Cleaver, and Wayne Smith, who have never won a significant professional title and probably never will, and who were watching the final round on TV along with all the hackers.

That's the game. Golf tournaments aren't won by the best shot or the best hole or the best round—or by the best swing or personality. They're won by the player who records the fewest strokes for seventy-two holes over four days, and there's a world of difference between that accomplishment and any of those others.